English
for International
Tourism

朗文旅游英语
初级·教师用书

U0107658

Elinor Ridler

南开大学出版社
天津

Pearson Education Limited
Edinburgh Gate
Harlow
Essex CM20 2JE
England
and Associated Companies throughout the world.

www.longman.com

First published 2003

Second impression 2003

ISBN 0 582 479908

Set in 10/12pt Times New Roman

Printed in Spain by Gráficas Estella

Acknowledgements

The author would like to thank Amanda Bailey, Iwonna
Dubicka, Philip Lamble, Margaret O'Keefe, Ian Wood
and all the staff at Pearson involved in the production of
this book for all their help and encouragement.

Images taken from DK Eyewitness Travel Guides
published by Dorling Kindersley Limited:

Travel Guide Amsterdam - page 83; Travel Guide
Barcelona - page 81 and 82

Designed by Jennifer Coles

Illustrated by Bill Donohoe

Contents

Introduction

Aims of the course

English for International Tourism Pre-intermediate is designed for people who need to improve their English because they are training to work or are already working in hotel or tourism industries. The course is intended for students who already have a basic knowledge of English. It is suitable for students studying in either a monolingual or a multilingual classroom situation.

The syllabus is multi-layered. Based on topic areas and professional skills relevant to the students, it also incorporates a related comprehensive grammar and vocabulary syllabus and systematic work on speaking, listening, reading and writing. It takes an integrated approach to pronunciation and includes revision.

Structure of the course

The course consists of a students' book, teacher's book, workbook and class cassette / CD. The students' book contains fifteen units. Each unit deals with an area of the hotel and tourism industry and related professional skills such as dealing with complaints, talking on the telephone, recommending sights and taking orders in a restaurant. In addition, each unit has a grammar and a lexical focus. After every five units there is a consolidation unit which can be used either for assessment of student progress or for revision. A summary of the unit contents can be found on pages 4–5 of the students' book.

The notes in the teacher's book are designed to help teachers use the material in the students' book most effectively and adapt it in terms of procedure, length or difficulty to suit their own classes. It includes explanations of terminology and references specific to the hotel and tourism industries for teachers not familiar with the subject. There is also a bank of photocopiable material on pages 79–94 of the teacher's book which can be used to extend or adapt a lesson, or for revision later.

Skills

The four skills – reading, writing, listening and speaking – are practised and developed in each unit of the coursebook. The teaching material comes from a wide range of sources related to the hotel and tourism industry, including the *Dorling Kindersley Eyewitness Travel Guides* (see page 5), travel- and tourism-related websites, travel brochures, journals and so on. The varied tasks in each unit are suited to the needs of hotel and tourism students, providing many opportunities for students to use their existing knowledge of the English language and the new input in a wide range of contexts relevant to their field.

The range of text types throughout the students' book reflects the industry and provides the students with practice in various real-life situations, from writing letters of apology and CVs to dealing with customers on the telephone, taking orders in a restaurant and giving presentations.

Listening: There are listening tasks in each unit. The listening extracts, which are on both cassette and CD, are again relevant to the industry, including dialogues between hotel staff and guests, and between travel agents and customers. The tapescripts for each extract are provided at the end of the coursebook on pages 132–143 and can be used to give extra support for less advanced listeners. They can also be used for self study, to check language and students can even listen and read the tapescript simultaneously.

Speaking: There is a strong focus on this skill throughout the course, as the ability to communicate well in the hotel and tourism industry is essential. There is a variety of speaking activities in the students' book, with extra suggestions for further speaking practice provided in the teacher's book. Students practise the language through realistic tasks and there is help with the appropriate language and level of professional formality that are necessary in different situations. The speaking tasks range from basic telephone dialogues to more complex problem-solving activities and formal presentations. The productive skills are further practised in the professional practice tasks (see page 5).

Reading: In both the students' book and the teacher's book, guidance is given on how to approach a text to improve students' reading skills. The tasks vary from one unit to the next. Further reading practice, which can be set for homework, is provided in the workbook.

Writing: In addition to accuracy and range of language used, students learn the importance of effective communication of message, style and organisation in formal and informal written documents. They are also given the opportunity to consolidate what they are learning by means of an ongoing course project, the travel guide project (see page 5).

Language

The language presented in the course is introduced and practised in context in both the students' book and the workbook. The language introduced in each unit is highlighted in the language focus boxes which appear throughout the students' book. The course provides a graded grammar syllabus combining language that is necessary for students at pre-intermediate level and language which occurs frequently in the hotel and tourism industry.

Vocabulary

New vocabulary, which is topic-based and directly related to the hotel and tourism industry, is generally introduced through the source materials. Students are given the opportunity to practise the words in a variety of tasks in both the students' book and the workbook. There are also tips in the students' book and teacher's book which help students to organise and learn the new vocabulary.

Professional practice

The course has a strong focus on students' developing professional skills. Each unit of the students' book has at least one professional task, the language and structure of which are provided in the professional practice boxes. The tasks are either spoken, such as selling a conference venue or persuading a client to buy a package tour, or written, such as writing a hotel description or a covering letter for a CV.

Pronunciation

There is a strong focus on pronunciation throughout the course, especially on intonation and stress patterns. It is easy for non-native speakers of English to sound unintentionally rude or aggressive as a result of inappropriate pronunciation. Over the course, students are made aware of the pronunciation features which help them to sound polite and enthusiastic. There are pronunciation tips and practice in the students' book, workbook and teacher's book.

Consolidation units

These extra units are designed to offer a diagnostic tool for the students' language development. They focus on the grammar and vocabulary from the previous four units, reviewing them in slightly different contexts. The exercises can be used selectively throughout the course or set as a test at the end of every five units.

Weblinks

Reference is made thoughout the teacher's book to useful weblinks. They can be used to find information in a variety of ways, depending on the school facilities and students' access to the internet, e.g. students can look up information in class or at home, or teachers can research sites and then print out information for use in class. The weblinks are particularly useful for finding more information about the topics and places in each unit and for researching information to include in the travel guide projects.

Google and *Ask Jeeves* are two search engines which provide an endless source of information. If you want to find information about any subject, just go to these search engines and ask for the information you require. They will then refer you to relevant websites. Give these weblinks to your students at the beginning of the course as they will help them when they need to research a topic during the course.

http://www.google.com
http://www.ask.com

Dorling Kindersley Eyewitness Travel Guides

The *Dorling Kindersley Eyewitness Travel Guides* are a series of illustrated travel guides which give extensive information about different destinations around the world. They provide detailed information on the history, culture and customs, sites, things to do, places to stay, places to eat and travel tips for the relevant city / country. Many of the reading texts in the students' book are taken from these guides, thus providing authentic texts for class use. The guides themselves also serve as a useful reference for teachers if they need more information about the destinations in the units. These guides are the basis for the travel guide project.

Travel guide project

As an integral part of the course, students are encouraged to write a travel guide for their own city or area. This guide is added to throughout the course and is based on the *Dorling Kindersley Eyewitness Travel Guide* features that are integrated into several units. The project can be done individually, in pairs or in small groups. It gives students the opportunity to consolidate language and vocabulary input in a personalised context. The teacher's book indicates when students should produce something for the project, what information they should include and how they might present the information.

All in a day's work

Fact File

Website: http://travel.dk.com

Unit notes

Before you start working on the unit ask your students what they know about the hospitality industry and whether they are interested in working in it. It is useful for you to get some ideas from them before you start. In this way you can see how much they know and what their interests are.

Exercise 1, page 6

Ask students to look at the pictures and give them a few minutes to think about the advantages and disadvantages of working in a hotel before comparing their answers with their partners and then with the rest of the class.

Possible advantages:
meet lots of people; it is interesting; lots of different jobs

Possible disadvantages:
hours are long and unsociable; usually work at weekends; guests may be difficult

Students will now be well prepared to do the next exercise.

Exercise 2, page 6

Tell students to scan the text and not to worry about detail at this stage.

b

Tell students to read the text in order to find the advantages and disadvantages of working in a hotel and then to compare them with their own ideas from exercise 1. Ask them whether they think the advantages outweigh the disadvantages.

Advantages:
fast-growing industry; exciting career; job satisfaction variety of jobs; paid sick leave and holidays; free food some free holidays; free or cheap accommodation

Disadvantages:
hard work, especially peak season; hours are long; seven-day week

Exercise 3, page 6

Now students need to read in more detail and may need help with some vocabulary. When they have found the answers, ask students to self-check in pairs first.

1 Housekeeper; management; administration jobs, e.g. accountant, marketing; concierge; porter.
2 Because it is not an easy job and the hours can be very long.
3 They are responsible for the rooms, food and beverage service, registration and general management.
4 Each job involves dealing with people.
5 *Exciting, hard* and *different*.

NB Students often make mistakes with *responsible* as the construction may be different in their own language. *Responsible* is neither a noun nor a job title in English.

Exercise 4, page 7

Before doing this exercise, look back at the answer to question 1 in exercise 3 and ask students to discuss in pairs what each job or area of work involves. In this way students have to think for themselves and it gives them a chance to share their knowledge about the different jobs. Ask them to do the vocabulary exercise in pairs so that they can discuss the jobs and help each other with unknown vocabulary.

1 b 2 d 3 e 4 h 5 g 6 a 7 c 8 f

Workbook homework: exercises 1 and 2, pages 4–5.

Exercise 5, page 7

Let students say each word and decide whether or not they can hear the /h/ sound. Then say each word yourself before checking answers as a class.

> The word which does not have this sound is *hours* /aʊəz/, /aʊrz/.

> **Extra Activity**
> Tell students to hold their hands in front of their mouths and to pronounce the words in the box. Try to elicit from them what they can feel when they say the words with the /h/ sound and what is different when they say *hours*.
>
> *Answer: when they pronounce the /h/ they can feel their breath on their hands while when they say* hours *they can feel nothing.*

Exercise 6, page 7

Give students a few minutes to write down their ideas before talking to their partners. Ask them to find out whether their ideas are the same and then to agree on the two best things.

Exercise 7, page 8

Before playing the CD / cassette, tell students to predict what her job may involve and what it would be like to work in the Caribbean. It is useful for students to have some ideas in mind before they listen.

As they will not be able to guess what SOs and COs are, tell them to focus only on this information. Play the CD / cassette twice if necessary and stop after each extract when they hear it for the second time.

See tapescript (students' book page 132).

> SOs = stay-overs
> COs = check-outs

Exercise 8, page 8

Before playing the recording again, ask students to predict what the job involves and to tick what they think is appropriate. They may also tick what they remember from the previous hearing.

> a, d, e, f, g

Exercise 9, page 8

Students can also try to predict the answers to this exercise. It would also be interesting to see what ideas students have about the industry and then to see whether they coincide with Darina's answers (they may be surprised).

See tapescript (students' book page 132).

> 1 Six days a week.
> 2 Always.
> 3 Tuesday or Wednesday.
> 4 From nine to three o'clock.

Once you have checked the answers, ask students to comment on Darina's working hours. *Are they good hours? Would you like to have a timetable like this?*

Workbook homework: exercise 4, page 6.

Language focus: Adverbs of frequency

Let students work out the rules themselves by looking at the examples. If they have any difficulties, put one example of each on the board and look at them together. Ask students where the adverb is in relation to the verb *be* and the other verb.

> We put adverbs <u>after</u> the verb *be* and <u>before</u> other verbs.

See grammar reference section (students' book page 125).

Exercise 10, page 8

Tell students that they are going to interview each other to find out how often their partner does various things. As they speak, they should take notes. Brainstorm the kind of things they can tell each other about: how often they go to the cinema, read, do sport, go abroad, etc. They need to find enough information to be able to write one sentence for each adverb. Depending on time, you could set the written part for homework.

Workbook homework: exercise 3, page 6.

Exercise 11, page 9

Students generally find listening and taking notes difficult even if they only have to write a few words. For this reason, they need to develop good habits. They should always read the questions very carefully before they listen, for example, so they know what kind of information to listen out for. As this is the first listening exercise like this in the book, read through the questions as a class and ask students what kind of word or words they will need to use in order to complete the information.

See tapescript (students' book page 132).

1 a number (write as a figure or a word) 2 a verb in the infinitive 3 a reason 4 a verb in the third person

They should also decide which ones will need more than one word.

Play the CD / cassette twice before asking them to compare their answers. If necessary play it a third time, stopping after each question to check the answer.

1 six, eight 2 train 3 can contact 4 checks

Language focus: Present simple

Although students should be familiar with this language point by now, it is a useful reminder to focus on the use of the auxiliary, the often-forgotten third person *s* and the irregular verbs (*have–has / do–does / finish–finishes*).

See grammar reference section (students' book page 125).

Exercise 12, page 9

This exercise is to practise and check the present simple in the form of an interview.

1 do you do 2 go 3 don't usually stay 4 is 5 do you do 6 visit 7 has 8 go 9 plays 10 Do you stay 11 don't stay 12 start 13 like 14 watch 15 don't do

Workbook homework: exercises 5–7, pages 6–7.

P Photocopiable extra, see page 79

This is a whole-class mingling activity in which students have to find someone who has the same job as them. Half the cards show the job title while the other half show the duties that each job involves. If you have more students than cards, make extra copies of some of the jobs and their corresponding duties.

Give each student either a job card or a duty card. Make sure that each student has a card that corresponds to another student's card. Give them time to think about what is written on their card, which they must not show to anyone else. Tell students that they have to find another student who does the same job as them by asking *yes / no* questions, for example if a student has a card which says *housekeeper* they should ask questions corresponding to this job, e.g.

Do you clean rooms? Do you change bedding and towels?

If a student has a duties card, they should find someone with the corresponding job card. *Are you a housekeeper?*

They should go around the class asking questions until they find their partner.

Extra Activity

The cards can also be used for a Pelmanism matching game. Divide the class into small groups. Give each group a copy of the jobs cards and duties cards, preferably stuck on thick card. Place all the cards with the writing face down. Students take it in turns to turn over first a duty card, then a job card to find the pairs. Before they pick up a job card, they have to say the name of the job. If they do not know the name, they cannot pick up the job card. If the cards do not match, turn them face down again after showing them to the other members of the group. If they find a matching pair, they keep both cards until the end of the game. The winner is the person with the most cards at the end.

Exercise 13, page 10

Now students talk about themselves. In order to complete the sentences, students need to work together and find out information about each other regarding the topics in the box. While they are speaking they should take notes so that they have the information ready when they write their sentences. When they have enough information, they can write their sentences and then report back to the class.

NB Students often have problems with what to do with the verb after *none of us*. In fact native speakers often disagree about this point too. In general, the verb can be either singular or plural. The singular is more formal while the plural is more informal.

Exercise 14, page 10

Introduce students to the individual sounds first. Say them yourself and ask them to repeat after you. Exaggerate the sounds to emphasise the difference between them. Then say each word in the box to help students put them in the appropriate groups. When they have finished grouping the words, ask students to repeat each word after you.

/s/	/z/	/ɪz/
starts, wants	goes, flies, arrives	watches, washes, finishes

Anthony Grey
Assistant Concierge

I've been here at the Sun Bay Hotel for two years and I really love my job. I greet guests at the door and sometimes I collect them and their luggage from the airport. What I like about my job is meeting all kinds of people and making friends. This is very important for me and my job gives me plenty of opportunities to do this.

Extra Activity

Ask students to work out the rules for themselves and then to add another verb to each group.
NB Not all the possibilities are here (see below for extra rules and examples).

Rules:
/s/ after verbs ending in /t/
/z/ after verbs ending in /aʊ/, /aɪ/ and /v/
/ɪz/ after verbs ending in /tʃ/ and /ʃ/

Extra rules and examples:
/s/ after /p/ and /k/, e.g. *stops, picks*
/ɪz/ after /ks/ and /s/, e.g. *fixes, kisses*
/z/ after all other endings, e.g. *needs, sees, sings*

Exercise 15, page 10

This exercise serves as preparation for the writing activity in exercise 16, providing students with a model to work from.

Ask students to look at the webpage and to comment on it. *Where would you find it? Who is it for? What other information would be on the site?* Students then read the webpage and answer the questions. As they answer the questions remind them to underline where they find the answers in the text.

1 F (she has been there since it opened) **2** T **3** T
4 F (every day is different)

Exercise 16, page 10

Before students start the exercise, elicit the questions they need to ask in order to complete the information. *What is his surname? What does he do? What's his job? What are his duties? What does he like about his job?*

Direct students to the pairwork files at the back of the book and remind them not to look at their partner's information. Once they have all the information, they write the texts with the help of the description about Vanessa. The texts should be in the first person as in the example and they should show enthusiasm about their jobs as they are promoting their hotel.

The texts may vary a little according to the ability of the students. While some students may only include the exact information given, others may be able to add a little more. When they have finished let each pair compare their texts with two other pairs to see how they can improve their own. If you have time, each group can then present their text as if they were Anthony and James.

Exercise 17, page 11

Ask students to look at the different countries and to see whether they can name each one before looking at the words in the box.

1 USA, US / American **2** Italy, Italian **3** Russia, Russian **4** France, French **5** Spain, Spanish **6** Germany, German

NB Tell students that we can write *USA* but we say *the USA*.

They may need help when writing the nationalities so, if necessary, let them use dictionaries or ask you.

We refer to different nationalities in the following ways:
the British   British people   people from Britain

Workbook homework: exercises 8–10, page 7.

Exercise 18, page 11

In this information gap activity students practise what they have studied in exercises 17 and 18 in order to complete the hotel registers. Tell them that they are each going to have half a hotel register which they need to complete by asking each other questions. Focus their attention on the questions they need to ask before turning to the relevant pages.

NB Students do not look at each other's information when they are doing this activity.

When the registers are complete, students check with each other whether all the information is correct. As you monitor the pairwork, make notes of any mistakes / problems that arise and spend a few minutes at the end going over them as a class.

② Fly-drive holidays

UNIT OBJECTIVES

Professional skills:	dealing with telephone enquiries and bookings
Language focus:	present continuous for future arrangements
Vocabulary:	car-hire expressions

Fact File

Dorling Kindersley Eyewitness Travel Guide Florida

Useful weblinks for general information about Florida:
http://travel.dk.com
http://www.lonelyplanet.com
http://www.thomascook.com
http://www.timeout.com

Give these travel guide weblinks to your students so that they can investigate Florida for themselves. These sites all have information about hotels, tourist attractions, means of travel, etc. all over the world. Students will need to log on to the main page, ask for specific information about Florida and take it from there.

Unit notes

Introduce students to the theme of the unit. Focus on the title and ask them what they think it means. Arouse interest by asking them what they know about Florida. *Has anyone been there? Would you like to go there on holiday? Why / why not?*

Fact File

Florida, otherwise known as the Sunshine State, is located on the east coast of the United States. Tourists are attracted there by its warm sunny climate, white sandy beaches, clear blue seas, the Kennedy Space Center and, of course, Disney World. The main cities in this state are Orlando and Miami.

Exercise 1, page 12

Use the pictures to prompt conversation. Tell students that the photos come from a real travel guide. Give them a few minutes to talk about the pictures in pairs and to comment on which places they would like to visit and what they think it would be like there. They then match the pictures to the places.

1 Daytona Beach **2** Kennedy Space Center **3** Universal Studios **4** Disney World Theme Park

Exercise 2, page 12

Before moving on to this exercise, ask students what information you need to give when booking a holiday, such as your name, destination, etc. Let them compare their answers with the information in their books. This will help them focus on the questions carefully before they listen. Let them listen twice before checking their answers with a partner.

See tapecript (students' book page 132).

1 f **2** d **3** a **4** b **5** c **6** e

Exercise 3, page 12

As they have already listened to the conversation, see whether students can answer any of the questions before listening again. Then play the CD / cassette before checking the answers as a class.

1 flight, accommodation and car hire **2** self-catering apartment and hotel **3** second half of May **4** number of nights, price per person **5** once a week / every Thursday **6** London Heathrow

Exercise 4, page 13

Students will need to listen again to complete the booking form. As before, they may be able to add some of the information before listening again.

1 self-catering apartment **2** 14 **3** Thursday 17 May **4** Thursday 31 May **5** 2 **6** Jane Wright, Simon Wright **7** 1 **8** Andrew Wright

Workbook homework: exercises 1–5, pages 8–9.

Professional practice, telephone enquires

These tips are to help students deal with customers. Before students look at the tips, elicit some of the phrases. Ask students what a travel agent should do on answering the phone, how they should sound, what they need to check, etc.

Now look at the professional practice box and see whether they were right. Look at the strategies as a class and practise saying the phrases in the appropriate way. This will set students up well for the pairwork activity in exercise 5. To help with pronunciation and intonation, students can repeat the phrases after you or listen and repeat from the CD / cassette.

Exercise 5, page 13

Now it is the students' turn to be the travel agent and customer. Divide the class into two groups. Half of them (A) are the travel agents and the other half (B) are the customers. If you have an odd number of students, one extra customer can join a pair and go to the travel agency as a couple. Ask them to read their respective instructions in the back of the book and to prepare their information in groups of three or four. Give them about ten minutes to prepare. When they are ready put them into A / B pairs to practise their dialogues.

NB Before they start, remind the travel agents that their customer will only book a holiday with them if they are treated well, so they need to take into account the strategies in the professional practice box. Tell the customers that as they make their enquiries, they should consider whether their travel agent is following the strategies and remember that they should only make their booking if they are satisfied with the service they have been given. At the end, see who has / has not booked a holiday and ask why / why not. *Did you feel that you were treated well? Were you given the information that you asked for? Was the service satisfactory?*

Exercise 6, page 14

This exercise shows what Florida has to offer tourists. Using the pictures as a prompt, ask students to discuss what you can do in Florida and whether it would make an interesting and varied holiday. Students then read the extract from the *Dorling Kindersley Eyewitness Travel Guide Florida* and answer the questions, giving reasons for their answers.

1 Disney World, Universal Studios, Sea World, Busch Gardens **2** Panhandle **3** Kennedy Space Center **4** Daytona International Speedway **5** Everglades National Park **6** Gold Coast **7** Universal Studios

Exercise 7, page 14

Tell students that Oscar is planning a trip to Florida and has sent an email to his friend Jackie who lives there. Students read the email and answer the questions.

1 a fortnight / two weeks **2** Orlando **3** July 15th **4** 7.45 am **5** at the airport

Extra Activity

Ask students about emails. *Do they use email? How much? Who to? What are the advantages / disadvantages?* Students look at Oscar's email and comment on its layout and style.

Exercise 8, page 15

Before playing the CD / cassette, give students some time to predict the answers in pairs. For more information on staging listening tasks, see page 4 of the introduction.

See tapescript (students' book pages 132–133).

The red line should go from Orlando airport to Disney World, then to Kennedy Space Center, the Everglades National Park, Miami and then straight up to the Panhandle.

1 It's late and she's going to bed.
2 By car.
3 She's working.
4 He's meeting another friend from college.
5 He's going to the Panhandle to relax on a beach.
6 Probably not! He's too busy.

For a follow-up discussion ask students what they think of Oscar and Jackie. *What is their relationship? Are they good friends? Do they want to see each other?*

Language focus: Present continuous

Refer students to the language focus box, paying special attention to the verbs not used in the continuous form.

See grammar reference section (students' book page 125).

Workbook homework: exercises 6–8, pages 10–11.

Exercise 9, page 15

This exercise is very structured and good for less advanced students. See alternative suggestion below for more advanced students. Ask students to plan a holiday for themselves by choosing a date, airport and sight. When they have planned their holidays, elicit what questions they should ask each other to talk about their plans. *When are you going? Which airport are you flying to? Which sights / places are you visiting? Who are you meeting?* Students should then mingle and try to find people who will be in the same place at the same time as themselves. Students can then report back to the class who they are going to meet on their holidays.

Extra Activity

The exercise can be extended by allowing students to choose sights from the *Florida at a glance* section on page 14 to plan their holidays. It gives them more freedom and flexibility to organise an interesting and varied holiday for themselves. To make the exercise work, though, they will still need to use one of the three airports marked on the map and the dates on page 15.

Exercise 10, page 15

Give students plenty of time to explore the websites and travel guide referred to in the introduction of the unit either in class or for homework. The holiday plan should be detailed with dates, sights, means of transport and activities.

Extra Activity

Students present their holidays to the class and they vote for the best / most varied holiday.

Travel guide project

Your country at a glance
Based on the *Florida at a glance* extract on page 14, students write a similar description of their area or a popular tourist region in their country. The text can be brief and they should include a map and pictures which they can obtain from the internet, the local tourist office or a travel agency.

Exercise 11, page 16

Tell students that they are going to hear a man phone a car hire company. Ask them to look first at the pictures of the cars and to decide which would be best for him and his family. Students should do this in small groups before discussing it as a class.

The luxury and sports utility vehicles because they have a lot of room, four doors and a big boot for family luggage. They are also probably safer.

Extra Activities

1 Ask students which car they would choose for a holiday to Florida with their friends.

2 This activity will set students up well for exercises 12 and 13 and personalises the theme of car hire. Ask students whether they have ever hired a car before. If someone has, ask them to tell the rest of the class about their experience of booking it. If not, ask them the following questions: *Where can you find information about hiring a car? What questions would you ask the car hire firm? What would be the most important factors for you when hiring a car?* Students answer these questions in pairs or small groups before sharing their ideas with the rest of the class.

Possible answers:
• in the local phone book / on internet / ask friends
• price, insurance, model of cars available, what is included in the price
• size of the car, price, number of doors, etc.

Exercise 12, page 16

Students can use dictionaries or ask you for help if necessary.

1 b 2 c 3 d 4 e 5 f 6 a

Check understanding by asking students to explain the expressions.

Fact File

Third-party liability is when you are insured against any damage you cause to other people and property. You are not insured for damage you cause to yourself or your hire car. In the USA, standard insurance includes only limited third-party liability so car hire companies recommend additional liability insurance (ALI) to non-Americans.
Collision damage waiver (*CDW*): this is extra insurance which covers you for any damage you may cause to the rental car itself.

Exercise 13, page 16

Ask students to read the instructions and sentences carefully. Make sure they understand what they have to do before they listen. Let students listen twice before comparing their answers.

1 a **2** c **3** f **4** e **5** d **6** b

Students discuss in pairs whether or not they think the agent was helpful and why / why not. They don't need to agree.

In some ways he is helpful: he gives lots of information and answers Mr Craig's questions, but his manner is abrupt, especially at the end when he puts the receiver down.

Workbook homework: exercise 9, page 11.

Exercise 14, page 17

Before students listen to the sentences, tell them that we usually stress the content words, that is the words which carry meaning. Students listen to the CD / cassette and then practise saying the sentences, paying attention to the stress patterns.

See tapescript (students' book page 133).

Professional practice: Making calls

Remind students that how you deal with clients on the phone and the language you use is extremely important. The strategies here will help students give the right impression when they are speaking to clients. Discuss the strategies with students and compare the expressions with those used when phoning in their own language. Give students time to practise saying the expressions so that they are well prepared for exercise 15.

Exercise 15, page 17

It is a good idea to spend time setting up this activity well before students practise the dialogue together as the better prepared they are, the better they will do the task. Tell students that it is their turn to speak on the phone and that they should follow the strategies in the professional practice box.

Divide the class into two groups. Half of the class work for World Breaks car rental (A) and the other half are customers (B). Students work together in their groups, using the information they have, and prepare any questions / expressions they will need to use in their phone conversation. Encourage them to use expressions from the previous exercises.

When students are ready, put them into A / B pairs to practise the conversation and to complete the missing information. Give them plenty of time to practise. Go around listening and helping them with language and pronunciation.

Table for two

Before focussing on the coursebook, introduce the subject of food and eating out. Brainstorm the food students like / dislike and where they prefer to eat: at home or out? With family or friends?

Unit notes

Exercise 1, page 18

Students look at the pictures and, while matching the dishes, comment on which ones they like / dislike, how often they eat them and whether or not they are popular in their country. Ask students to choose their top five national dishes.

1 seafood **2** roast beef **3** Phanaeng curry **4** banana split **5** spaghetti

Exercise 2, page 18

After students have shared their information in pairs, put them in groups of four. Tell students that they will work together to combine their information in the form of a survey, as they did in unit 1 exercise 13, using these expressions: *all of us, two of us, one of us, none of us.*

Exercise 3, page 18

Students will know some of the words but might need dictionaries for words like *cod*.

Fish	Meat	Vegetables	Fruit
salmon	chicken	peas	banana
tuna	beef	potatoes	orange
cod	lamb	carrots	apple

Extra words: give students a limit to the number of words they add, such as two for each category. They can always add more for homework.

Remind students that there are sometimes silent letters in English. Ask them which two food items have a silent letter: *salmon* /ˈsæmən/ and *lamb* /læm/.

Exercise 4, page 18

Ask whether anyone likes cooking. If they do, what are their specialities? As they look at the pictures, ask students which things they know how to make. Then match the words.

1 boil **2** bake **3** fry **4** roast **5** stuff **6** grill

Students may have different ideas or preferences for what you can do with the food in exercise 3. If they are interested in this topic, give them time to talk at some length about food, cooking, likes and dislikes.

Possible answers:
You can:
- fry, grill, boil and bake fish
- fry, roast, grill most meat and also stuff chicken
- fry, roast, boil, bake, stuff and grill various vegetables
- fry and bake some fruit

Exercise 5, page 19

Before looking at the menus themselves, ask students what a menu is and what they would expect to find on menus in general. Try to elicit *starters*, *main courses* and *desserts*. In pairs, students decide where the menus come from, giving reasons for their answers. Tell them not to worry about what everything means yet, as this will be dealt with in exercises 6 and 7.

The word *menu* is a false friend in some languages. If necessary, remind students that a *menu* is a list of dishes offered by a bar / restaurant in the form of a document or on a board, and not another word for a *set meal*.

1 c (*Please pay for your food when you order at the bar*)
2 b (not much choice)

Fact File

Pub lunches are very popular in Britain. Families often eat in pubs at weekends and many people spend their lunch break from work in the pub. The choice and quality of pub food varies greatly but in general it is good and prices are reasonable. Some pubs also serve food in the evening which is cheaper than in a restaurant.

Exercise 6, page 19

All the phrases are in the menus so ask students to underline them as this will help them to complete the exercise. Students can then do the exercise in pairs and should refer to the menus and to exercise 4 (for *roast* and *bake*, etc.) if necessary.

1 b 2 f 3 d 4 e 5 a 6 c

Exercise 7, page 19

First ask students which dishes they can find on the menus and which dishes they recognise. As some of these dishes may be unfamiliar to them, it is better to do this exercise as a class and for students to match the ones they know first before focussing on the unknown dishes. Elimination is often a good way to find answers.

1 b 2 f 3 c 4 e 5 a 6 d

Workbook homework: exercises 1 and 2, pages 12–13.

Exercise 8, page 19

Give students a few minutes to discuss their choices in pairs or small groups.

Language focus: Countable and uncountable nouns

Focus students' attention on the box. They should work out the answers by reading the example sentences.

- You <u>can</u> count countable nouns.
- You <u>cannot</u> count uncountable nouns.
- You <u>cannot</u> use *a* or *an* before an uncountable noun.

See grammar reference section (students' book page 126).

Exercise 9, page 20

As students can find the concept of countable and uncountable nouns confusing, do some examples on the board. Choose some words in the list and ask students which group they belong to and why. Possible problems:

spaghetti (in some languages it is a countable noun, in English it is not); *coffee* (the substance) and *a coffee* (a cup of coffee); *milk* (liquid) but *a bottle of milk*. Let students work out the answers for themselves before explaining in detail how some food items can be both countable and uncountable (see separate box).

- countable: meal, prawn, sandwich, vegetable
- both: aubergine, chicken, chocolate, coffee, curry, juice, lettuce, omelette, potato, pizza, salad, salmon, sugar, tomato, fruit
- uncountable: broccoli, food, milk, rice, salt, spaghetti

UK vs. US: in the UK people say *aubergine*, while in the US they say *eggplant*. The pronunciation of tomato varies too: /təˈmɑːtəʊ/ (UK), /təˈmeɪtoʊ/ (US).

Workbook homework: exercise 3, page 14.

Exercise 10, page 20

This is a very useful exercise as some food vocabulary is difficult to pronounce. Make sure students know what the boxes represent before you start the exercise (they represent the number of syllables in each word and the big box shows where the main stress falls). Knock on the board or clap your hands to demonstrate each pattern. Elicit one food item from exercise 9 for each group before they complete the exercise in pairs.

When they listen to check their answers, give them enough time to make any necessary changes and ask them to repeat after each one.

See tapescript (students' book page 133).

■	■ ■	■ ■ ■	■ ■ ■
rice	chocolate	vegetable	potato
juice	omelette	aubergine	spaghetti
milk	coffee	broccoli	tomato
salt	salmon		
prawn	sugar		
fruit	chicken		
meal	sandwich		
food	lettuce		
	pizza		
	salad		
	curry		

Workbook homework: exercise 7, page 15.

Language focus: *Some* and *any*

As before, students work out the answers from the examples.

> * *some* in positive sentences, offers and requests
> * *any* in negatives and questions
> * *some* and *any* with plural countable and uncountable nouns

See grammar reference section (students' book page 126).

Exercise 11, page 21

Students can refer to the language focus for help and then check in pairs. They should be prepared to explain the reason for their answers.

> **1** some **2** a **3** some **4** any **5** some, any **6** any **7** a
> **8** a, some

Workbook homework: exercise 4, page 14.

Exercise 12, page 21

Before looking at the tips in the students' book, introduce the topic of recording and learning vocabulary. Ask students whether they find it easy or difficult to learn, how they record it and whether they have any tips. Students discuss it in pairs and then report back to the class.

Students look at the illustrations and at the written ideas and discuss them. Tell them to choose the two which are the most useful for them. Spend some time with feedback as this is an important area for learners. Useful extra vocabulary includes: *check, revise, look up a word, write down a word, write a definition.*

> ### Extra Activity
> Ask students to follow two of the tips over the next two weeks and to report back on how effective they have been in their learning. Spend part of a class on the feedback and encourage students to continue being systematic in their vocabulary recording.

Exercise 13, page 21

The information they find will depend on how good their dictionaries are. Tell students that it is worth their while investing in a good one, such as the *Longman WordWise Dictionary*. Tell them to look for the part of speech, pronunciation and definition of each word or leave it up to them to decide which information they need to know. They can then decide how they want to store these new words, with a picture or a definition in their notebooks.

Exercise 14, page 21

Depending on resources, this exercise can be done in class time or for homework. If students do not have access to the web, they can use recipe books or their own knowledge of their traditional dishes. Students can present their information in the form of a menu, recipe or oral presentation to the rest of the class or in groups.

The website www.recipesource.com has an extensive source of recipes from around the world. Students may find it interesting to browse around and find interesting recipes from other countries too.

P Photocopiable extra, see page 80

In this exercise students practise describing food and restaurant vocabulary in order to complete word puzzles and find the mystery food item.

Divide class into two groups. Give a copy of the A puzzles to one group and the B puzzles to the other group. In the A / B groups, students check the meanings of the food vocabulary that they are given in their half of the crossword. Make sure that they know the meaning of each word before putting them into pairs.

Put students into pairs consisting of one student from group A and one from group B. Tell them to sit face-to-face and that they cannot look at each other's answers. Student A describes each word in their puzzle. When B guesses the word, they write it in their empty puzzle. If they do not know how to spell a word, they can ask for the spelling. When B has guessed all the words and found the mystery food item, they change over and B describes their words to A.

At the end A and B compare answers to make sure that the words are all spelled correctly.

Travel guide project

What to eat in my country
Students add their recipes / menus to their projects using pictures from cookery books and giving descriptions in English of what the dish is and how it is served.

Language focus: *Much, many, a lot (of)*

Students work out the answers from the examples given.

> * We use *much* in questions and negative sentences with uncountable nouns.
> * We use *many* in questions and negative sentences with countable nouns.
> * We use *a lot* in positive sentences with both countable and uncountable nouns.

Exercise 15, page 22

Make sure students read the whole text before filling in the gaps. Ask them whether they have ever eaten Mexican food. *Did you like it? If you haven't tried it, would you like to?* Once they have completed the gaps and checked their answers, students practise the dialogue in pairs.

> **1** a lot of **2** much / a lot of **3** many / a lot of
> **4** a lot of **5** many **6** much / a lot **7** a lot of

Workbook homework: exercise 5, page 14.

Exercise 16, page 22

Tell students to read the introduction to the listening exercise and ask them whether they have ever complained in a restaurant. If they have, ask them to describe what the problem was and how it was solved. If not, ask them to think about what customers might complain about. If someone in the class has worked as a waiter or in a bar, ask them whether they have had complaints from customers. It would be interesting to hear both sides of the story.

Tell students before they listen to the three extracts that they only have to listen for the problem and need not worry about other details yet.

See tapescript (students' book pages 133–134).

> **1** The bill: the customers only had one bottle of water but were charged for two.
> **2** The slow service: they have been waiting for a long time.
> **3** The food: the steak is too rare and then overdone.
>
> NB Students do not need to use the exact words in their answers.

Exercise 17, page 22

Give students enough time to read through the statements before they listen again. Students discuss their answers in pairs before class feedback.

> **1** T **2** F (only one) **3** T **4** T **5** F (she has not served them at all) **6** F (he complains the steak is rare) **7** T

Students discuss the conversations in pairs and comment on the behaviour of the customers and the waiters. *Do you think that the waiters behaved appropriately? What would you have done?*

Professional practice: Dealing with complaints

Look at this with the students and emphasise that it is not only what you say, but how you say it that matters. Remind them that in this industry being polite is very important even if the customer is angry or being difficult. Remember: 'the customer is always right'.

Exercise 18, page 23

Give students a few minutes to look at the illustrations in pairs and to comment on what the problem is in each one before doing the exercise. Ask them to imagine what each person is saying without looking at the complaints given. Help them with unknown words as they come up.

> **1** c **2** a **3** b **4** e **5** d

> ### Extra Activity
> Ask students what they would do in these situations if they were a) the customer or b) the waiter. Remind students that they could find themselves in these situations one day!

Language focus: Complaining about food

Draw students' attention to the position of *too* and *enough* in the sentences. Also check the pronunciation of *enough* /ɪˈnʌf/.

Exercise 19, page 23

To set up this role-play, refer students back to the complaints in exercise 18 and the language focus. Also highlight the useful phrases at the bottom of the page, checking that they know what the expressions mean. Students look at the pictures and role-play the situations that they illustrate. They can take it turns to be the guest and the waiter so that they practise both roles. Remind students how important it is to be polite, however difficult the guests are. Students then act out their dialogues in front of the class.

NB If you have an odd number of students, make one group of three with two guests and one waiter.

Workbook homework: exercise 6, page 15.

> ### Extra Activity
> Ask students whether they would like to work as a waiter and if so, what kind of place would they like to work in, e.g. a restaurant, a luxury hotel, a beach resort, etc. *What do / don't they like about this profession? What are the advantages and disadvantages of it? Is it a hard job? What qualities do you need in order to be a good waiter?*

City tours

UNIT OBJECTIVES

Professional skills:	dealing with the public
Language focus:	past simple, *wh-* questions, prepositions of place
Vocabulary:	places of interest, prepositional phrases

Fact File

Dorling Kindersley Eyewitness Travel Guide Barcelona

Websites with information about Barcelona and tours around the city:
http://travel.dk.com
www.timeout.com/barcelona/
www.bcn.es/english/ihome.htm

Unit notes

Fact File

Barcelona, which is located on the east coast of Spain, is one of the most popular holiday and weekend destinations in Europe. Its popularity has increased greatly since it was host to the Olympic Games in 1992. Barcelona is a modern, cosmopolitan and cultural city which offers a wide range of attractions for visitors of all ages and backgrounds. Tourists are attracted by its varied architecture, especially buildings designed by Gaudí, and museums, the most popular of which is the Picasso Museum.

Many people go to Barcelona to enjoy its warm climate, local beaches and relaxed atmosphere. Another main attraction is the local football team, Barça, one of the top European teams.

Exercise 1, page 24

Find out what students know about Barcelona. If nothing else, most of them will probably know that the Olympics were held there in 1992 and some may know the famous football team, Barça. Students look at the pictures and make their choices for each group of tourists, giving their reasons for their choices.

Suggested answers:
Bus tour: a young couple, a couple in their 50s
Football Club: a family with young children, a couple in their 50s
Beach: students, a family with young children
Café: everyone

Fact File

La Rambla is the most famous avenue in the city and the number one tourist spot. It is a long avenue bordered by trees, with cafés, street musicians, human statues and stalls selling flowers and newspapers. It is busy at all times of day and night. The atmosphere is pleasant but beware of thieves as it is also the number one spot for pickpockets, who take advantage of tourists distracted by all the surrounding activities.

Exercise 2, page 24

Give students enough time to talk and find out each other's preferences before reporting to the class.

Exercise 3, page 24

Tell students that the first reading task is to read for gist, so they should not spend too much time deciding which title is most suitable.

The life of Antoni Gaudí is the best title as we learn a lot of information abut the architect himself.

Exercise 4, page 24

This time students need to read for more detail. Encourage them to use their own words where possible when giving their answers, rather than lifting the exact words from the text. Paraphrasing is a useful skill for language learners.

1 *La Pedrera* (*Casa Milá*), *Palacio Güell, Sagrada Familia* and *Parc Güell*.
2 Only the *Sagrada Familia*.
3 From after mass at 7 am to 6 or 7 pm.
4 He was dirty and was wearing old clothes. No one knew who he was.
5 He hated straight lines and wanted to show features and shapes of nature.

Exercise 5, page 25

Students refer to the text again to find why the dates are important. Remind students of the appropriate time prepositions which they should use in their answers. When the comprehension questions are all checked, students discuss Gaudí in small groups, commenting on his lifestyle and his architecture (using the illustrations to help). *Do you like his work?*

- In 1852 Gaudí was born.
- In 1909 he started work on the *Sagrada Familia*.
- From 1890 to 1904 he worked on *Parc Güell*.
- On 7 June 1926 he was hit by a tram.
- On 10 June 1926 he died.

Workbook homework: exercise 1, pages 16–17.

Exercise 6, page 25

This exercise will probably require some research by the students. Make it into a project and give it to them for homework so that they have a chance to check books or the internet for information. If their country has a number of famous architects, each group can choose, or be given, an architect to research. They can present their architect to the rest of the class as if they were tour guides giving information to tourists.

NB Tell students not to copy or translate directly from the material they find; they should present it in their own words.

Fact File

Students should be able to find information about their chosen architect by going to the following search engines and entering the name of the architect.
www.google.com
www.ask.co.uk
These search engines are a mine of information and extremely useful when looking for information about any subject.

Extra Activity

You can combine this exercise with exercise 10 on page 27 and follow it with a speaking activity in which students talk about the kind of buildings / architecture they prefer and which buildings they like best in their town / country.

Travel guide project

Star sights in my country
Students add the information they have found about an architect to their projects. They should add pictures of the architect's works and a brief biography.

Workbook homework: exercise 2, page 17.

Language focus: Past simple

Ask students which tense is used in the text about Gaudí. *Why is this tense used?* Students check their answers with the information in the language focus box. It is worth students underlining all the verbs in the past simple at this stage. Look through the box together and check that they understand the explanation. Refer students to the list of irregular verbs in the students' book (page 131). Some will already be familiar to them at pre-intermediate level but suggest that they revise the ones they know and learn the new ones. Choose ten examples, set them for homework and check them in the next class. Continue setting ten examples for homework until students have learned all the irregular verbs in the list.

Highlight the use of the auxiliary + infinitive in the negative and interrogative, as this is where students often make mistakes. Also check the spelling of past simple verbs whose infinitives end in -*y* (e.g. *played* vs. *tried*) and verbs that double the consonant in the past simple (e.g. *stopped*).

- Regular verbs: *worked, walked, tried, recognised, refused, discovered, moved, died, asked, hated, wanted*
- Irregular verbs: *was born, built, got up, ate, didn't eat, was, had, hit, took*

See grammar reference section (students' book page 126).

Exercise 7, page 26

As students have a tendency always to pronounce the -*ed* as an extra syllable, they need to know that this is not always correct. Do some examples on the board before starting the exercise, in order to highlight this. Make sure that students know the difference between the endings before they listen. Pronounce them individually and ask students to repeat after you. It helps students to know that the /d/ is a softer sound than the /t/ and that the /ɪd/ is an extra syllable. Read the words out loud. After checking that the words are in the right groups, students listen again and practise the pronunciation.

/t/	/d/	/ɪd/
worked	moved	hated
walked	refused	wanted
finished	discovered	needed
	lived	
	opened	

Extra Activity

Students work out the rule for themselves.

/t/   after verbs ending in *k*, *sh* (also *x* and *tch*)

/ɪd/   after verbs ending in *t* or *d*

/d/   all other regular verbs

Exercise 8, page 26

Students complete the exercise with the help of the irregular verb list on page 131 of the students' book if necessary. Tell them to look out for negatives and interrogatives in the sentences.

1 moved **2** Did you go, were **3** ate **4** wanted, took **5** bought, went **6** didn't have, was **7** asked **8** didn't understand, refused **9** walked, were **10** Did you see, visited

Workbook homework: exercises 3–5, page 18.

Exercise 9, page 27

Look at the pictures before doing the exercise and spend a few minutes talking about the pictures and what they represent. Depending on students' interest in football, see what else they know about the club and compare it to their own favourite team. Talk about star players either in their favourite team or in general, ask them whether any big championships are coming up and discuss who they think will win. Before they fill in the verbs, it is a good idea to encourage them to read the whole text so that they get a general idea of the contents.

Extra Activity

Give them some comprehension questions to give them a reason for reading the text to the end. By doing this you focus students on the *meaning* of the text before they work on the language.

Suggested true / false questions:
- FC Barcelona won their first ever match.   F
- They moved to their new stadium in 1899.   F
- The name of their stadium is *Nou Camp*.   T
- There is a museum at the stadium.   T
- Nou Camp is the largest stadium in the world.   F

---

1 played **2** lost **3** lived **4** moved **5** didn't move **6** needed **7** wasn't **8** took **9** had **10** gave **11** opened **12** were

Exercise 10, page 27

For this exercise, either follow the same steps as in exercise 6 or ask students to work on it individually. They can also use material from the appropriate tourist office. Encourage students to present their written material well, with illustrations and good, clear layout. When they give their oral presentations, as in exercise 6, they should imagine that the other students are tourists and let them ask questions after the presentation.

Exercise 11, page 28

Introduce the subject of tour guides. Ask students whether they have ever been on a guided tour anywhere. *Did you enjoy it? Do you think it is a good way to see a place or do you prefer to wander around using a guide book?* Give students enough time to discuss and make a note of the possible difficulties of the job. Ask them whether they think it is an easy / enjoyable job and whether they think they would like to do it. Make a note of their responses as you will need to refer back to them at the end of the unit.

Possible answers:
- people not listening or being unable to hear well
- people not understanding the language
- people not being interested
- the guide not being able to answer the questions that tourists ask them
- tourists being late or getting lost, complaints, etc. If students don't have many ideas themselves, give them some suggestions.

Ask students what they would do in those situations and which situations they think are the most usual / difficult.

Exercise 12, page 28

Before listening, look at the list of problems and see which ones the students mentioned in exercise 11. Students listen twice before checking answers.

See tapescript (students' book page 134).

1, 2, 3, 6

A *pickpocket* is a person who steals from people in public places, usually without the victim noticing. They take things from people's pockets and bags. Check pronunciation: *fountains* /ˈfaʊntənz/.

Workbook homework: exercises 7 and 8, page 19.

Exercise 13, page 28

Check that students know the meaning of all the question words before doing the matching exercise. Sometimes there is more than one possibility.

1 Where 2 When 3 How long 4 How much
5 Why 6 What 7 Who

Extra Activity

Either by listening once more or from what they remember, students then answer the questions in the exercise.

1 In Plaça d'Espanya.
2 In 1992.
3 About half an hour.
4 It's free.
5 Because of pickpockets.
6 By 10.15 pm.
7 A boy.

Exercise 14, page 29

Check that students understand the prepositions before doing the exercise. After checking the answers, students practise the prepositions by giving directions to places in their town or in the class / school.

1 On 2 in, opposite 3 near 4 up 5 straight ahead
6 from 7 in 8 over there

Exercise 15, page 29

In the dialogue there are lots of useful expressions which the students will need to use in exercise 17. As well as underlining the expressions in the tapescript, it is a good idea if they make a separate list which they can use as a quick reference when preparing their own tours.

- And on your left / right you can see …
- Now our next stop …
- The … was / were built in …
- Let me see …
- Please be back at the bus by …
- This area is known as …
- Please be careful of …
- Here we are.
- No … is allowed.
- If you would like some refreshments …
- This is the last stop on our tour …
- Please be ready by …

Workbook homework: exercise 6, page 19.

Exercise 16, page 29

Let students discuss their opinions in small groups and tell them that they do not need to agree with each other. They may have different opinions about this but in general she did give a good tour. Apart from not knowing when the fountains were built, she gave lots of information, answered the tourists' questions and her manner was polite and enthusiastic.

Exercise 17, page 29

Now it is the students' turn. This exercise can be done as a project with preparation done in class, combined with students bringing information from outside sources. Suggest that they go to the local tourist office if there is one or that they explore their area for themselves. Give them enough time to gather the information they need before preparing the tour itself in class. They will probably need a week or so to collect the information and a few classes to put their tours together.

When they have worked out their tour, tell them to think about how they are going to present it to tourists and which expressions they will need to use from exercise 15. They should then elect one or two people from their group to be the guide(s) who can practise giving the tour to the group before presenting it to the rest of the class. Mix more and less advanced students for this exercise.

Travel guide project

A bus tour
Students can add the bus tours to their projects with maps of the routes that the tours take and notes describing the sights along the routes.

Exercise 18, page 29

Before students start, check the tip box on page 29 for the guides and exercise 13 for the tourists. Emphasise the importance of being polite and enthusiastic in this industry. What's more, if you are polite and enthusiastic, your customers are more likely to be so too. During the tour, the tourists should think about whether the guide is following the tips.

To make the situation more authentic, arrange the classroom as if it were a bus, with the tourists all seated and the tour guide standing at the front. If you have access to a microphone, this would also add to the authenticity of the role-play.

Feedback after all the tours have been given will be useful for everyone; this can come from the 'tourists' themselves. Students can (a) vote for the tour they would prefer to go on, taking into account how interesting and varied it is, and (b) vote for the tour guide(s) they would prefer to have, taking into account the 'PIE' tips.

> ### Extra Activity
> For more advanced students, make it more challenging by 'planting' some difficult tourists on their tour or creating other problems which they will have to deal with without any planning. Give the 'tourists' cue cards with their roles on: for example, one tourist does not understand very well, another keeps asking difficult questions, the bus breaks down and people complain, etc. Point out that sometimes they may have to improvise: things do not always go according to plan, so these extra difficulties are useful practice for them.

P Photocopiable extra, see page 81

Giving directions

Students complete places on a map of Barcelona by asking for and giving directions.

Before they start, elicit questions to ask when you need directions, e.g.

Excuse me, where's the …?

Excuse me, can / could you tell me where … is, please?

Also elicit prepositions from exercise 14.

Divide class into A / B pairs and give them their corresponding maps. Tell them that they each have a map of Barcelona with different places marked on them. They imagine they are tourists asking for directions to the places written below their maps. They ask each other where these missing places are and put them on their map until they know where each place is. When both maps are complete, they compare maps to check answers. Make sure that they do not look at each other's maps to find the answers.

> ### Extra Activity
> Ask students whether they would now feel confident being a bus tour guide and whether they would like doing this job. Students give their reasons why / why not. Remind them of the comments they made in exercise 11. *Do they feel the same as they did then?*

Water cities

UNIT OBJECTIVES

Professional skills: describing hotels and facilities, dealing with new words
Language focus: comparatives and superlatives
Vocabulary: adjectives of description, accommodation and hotel facilities

Fact File

Dorling Kindersley Eyewitness Travel Guide Venice & the Veneto
Dorling Kindersley Eyewitness Travel Guide Amsterdam
http://travel.dk.com

Unit notes

Introduce the topic of hotels by asking students whether they have ever stayed in a hotel. If so, ask them to describe it / them; if not, what kind of hotel would they like to stay in?

Fact File

Both Venice, in the north of Italy, and Amsterdam, in the Netherlands, are well known for being cities built on water. Tourists who visit these two places enjoy boat tours on the waterways through the cities. Venice attracts tourists who are particularly interested in art and architecture and is a popular destination for couples who are looking for a short romantic break. Amsterdam is also rich in art and museums and one of the most popular tourist activities is to sit in the many street cafés and soak up the atmosphere.

Exercise 1, page 30

Students look at the different hotels and describe them in pairs, saying whether they would like to stay in them as well as answering the set questions. There are no specific answers so students can give their ideas freely.

NB Before deciding which star ratings to give the hotels, check that students know what the star ratings are, i.e. 1–5 stars, and that they have a general idea of what these hotels offer. They do not need to know exactly what each category has to offer at this stage.

Exercise 2, page 30

Tell students that the guests they are going to hear do not refer specifically to the hotels in exercise 1, but talk about the kind of places they would like to stay at. Students decide from the guests' comments and preferences which hotel is most suitable for each one. Their answers may vary but as long as they can justify their choice, accept it. Students should listen twice, then check in pairs before comparing with the rest of the class.

See tapescript (coursebook page 134).

Suggested answers:
- Guest 1 Londra Palace (first class and smart)
- Guest 2 Pensione Do Pozzi (quiet and there's a courtyard)

Exercise 3, page 30

Some of the vocabulary will be new to students so make this exercise into dictionary work. Some words can be used more than once. Check the meanings of all the expressions by asking students to give short definitions when checking the answers.

1 b 2 f 3 c 4 h 5 a 6 d 7 i 8 e 9 g

When students do a matching exercise like this, it is more useful for them to write out the whole expression in their notebooks or on cards rather than just to put **1 b**, **2 f**, etc. or to connect the answers with arrows. They are more likely to remember the expressions and they also have an organised record when they need to refer back to it.

Extra Activity

As the words in exercise 3 are quite long, students may have problems with word stress. They can either use their dictionaries to find where the main stress falls or they can listen to your example and mark the main stress on each set of words.

Exercise 4, page 30

Give students a couple of minutes to make a note of the most important hotel facilities for them. They do not have to consider only those mentioned in exercise 3. Students then compare in groups and give reasons for their choices. Referring back to the introduction, ask them whether the places where they normally stay have the five facilities that they have chosen.

Exercise 5, page 31

Tell students that they are going to read descriptions of different categories of hotels, one of each star rating. As there is a lot of information to read, give students enough silent reading time to make their matches. They will need to read all five descriptions before matching. The first time they read, suggest that they consider which hotels offer the most / least and which are more / less basic. This will help them to decide how many stars they each have. Students give reasons for their answers.

Extra Activity

To save time, either if the students are slow readers or if you do not have much time to spend on this exercise, divide the class into groups. Each group is given a star category and chooses which hotel best suits their category. This makes feedback interesting as each group explains their choice to the rest of the class. If different groups have chosen the same hotel, they discuss together which one is most appropriate, justifying their choice, or the other groups decide which one is the most suitable.

---

1 four star **2** five star **3** one star **4** two star
5 three star

Exercise 6, page 31

It is useful if students highlight the different groups of words in different ways, e.g. underline the room facilities, circle the hotel facilities, etc., so that class feedback is easier and more efficient. Put all their answers on the board divided up into four groups. Students should then note down the examples in the same way, thus giving them a clear reference.

1 en suite bath / shower, direct-dial telephone, hairdryer, toiletries, room service, colour TV, satellite TV
2 porter service, restaurant, laundry and dry-cleaning
3 well trained, attentive, efficient, courteous, professional
4 larger, small, medium sized, comfortable, well equipped, practical, spacious, simple, fully equipped

Workbook homework: exercises 1–3, pages 20–21.

Exercise 7, page 31

This speaking activity depends on students' knowledge of local hotels. If they know little about them, set them homework to go to some hotels and ask for information there or to find information at the local tourist office. When they have enough information, students discuss the

hotels in small groups. Alternatively, students can talk about the best hotel(s) they have ever stayed at: where they were, what they were like and what was so special about them.

Exercise 8, page 32

Ask whether anyone has stayed in a two-star hotel. *What was it like? What facilities did it have?* If not, look at the box and students decide which facilities they would find. They can refer back to the text on page 31 to check.

en suite shower room

Exercise 9, page 32

Students read the instructions to the listening exercise. Check that they understand the meaning of *upgrading* (when a hotel makes changes and improvements to raise its star rating). Ask why hotels might want to make these changes. Before playing the CD / cassette, look at the things that Renee will mention. Ask students to discuss them in pairs and to comment on how these things will improve the hotel. Students now listen and put them in order.

See tapescript (students' book page 134).

1 minibar and colour TV **2** fully-equipped bathrooms
3 reception area **4** bar **5** 24-hour room service
6 food service

Exercise 10, page 32

Give students some time to read everything and to make as many complete sentences as possible before listening again. When they listen they can check their answers and complete any sentences they have not done already.

1 b **2** a **3** g **4** f **5** e **6** c **7** d

Language focus: Comparatives and superlatives

Students complete the information in the language box using the examples in exercise 10 for help. Focus students on comparing equals and irregular adjectives, as mistakes are often made with these points.

- Comparative: add *-er*
- Superlative: add *-est*
- *big, bigger, biggest*
- Comparative: put *more* before the adjective
- Superlative: put *the most* before the adjective

See grammar reference section, page 127.

Exercise 11, page 33

As this is quite a difficult exercise, less advanced groups may need more guidance to complete the gaps. First look at the illustrations and discuss the various forms of transport: students describe what they are and compare them using different comparative and superlative forms. Students also compare them to transport in their own town / city and decide which is better. This will give them ideas and help them to do the exercise. Before focussing on the gaps, focus on the content of the text. Give students some comprehension questions or true / false statements to take them through the text.

How many different ways of getting around Amsterdam are mentioned in the text? (Five.)

Where can you buy tram and bus tickets? (On trams, on buses, tourist offices and newsagents.)

Who has priority on the roads: cyclists or tram drivers? (Tram drivers.)

Now they can complete the gaps.

For less advanced students, break the text down further and decide as a class what form is necessary in each gap before they write down the answers.

1 the most convenient **2** the most popular **3** easier **4** further **5** the cheapest **6** bigger than **7** The best **8** not as safe as **9** more enjoyable than / as enjoyable as **10** more suitable

Once the exercise is completed, ask students what they think of transport in Amsterdam. *Does it sound good? How would you like to travel around if you went there?*

Travel guide project

Getting around my city
Students write similar descriptions of the various types of transport in their city / town. They should compare the different types and comment on the best, cheapest and most popular ones and make recommendations for tourists visiting the town. They should also inlcude pictures of local buses, trams, trains, etc.

Exercise 12, page 33

Students can refer back to the information they gathered in exercise 7 to make the comparisons. Discuss in pairs or small groups which hotel is the best / worst / cheapest, etc., taking into account all the different points.

Exercise 13, page 34

In pairs, students brainstorm positive adjectives that they can use in their own language to make a hotel sound really attractive. Ask for two adjectives per pair. Students then translate them into English, using dictionaries if necessary. Put them on the board and see how much variety there is. Doing it in this way means that students have the chance to think of interesting words, rather than being limited by their knowledge of adjectives in English. Highlight the importance of using very positive language and a variety of adjectives when trying to create an impression in a sales environment. Check that students know the meanings of the words before they start matching.

1 high-class, spacious, excellent, modern
2, 3 attractive / charming / delightful
4 famous, impeccable, historic
5 value for money

Extra Activity
Students rewrite the text using the alternative vocabulary, then compare the new text with the original to see how much more impressive the new description sounds.

Travel guide project

My city's best hotels
For homework, students write descriptions of hotels in their city / area using the new vocabulary, making them sound as attractive as possible. Once students have written their descriptions of the hotels, they can practise reading them out and carefully pronouncing the positive adjectives in a suitable manner to 'sell' the hotel. Make sure that the students record the vocabulary in an organised way, with similar meanings together.
Add the descriptions to their projects with pictures to illustrate them.

Professional practice: Dealing with new words

Students often ask their teacher the meaning of every word they do not know, rather than trying to work it out for themselves. This may be due to laziness or lack of skill. Students need to be encouraged to look for clues to help them guess the meaning of new vocabulary. They generally want to know the exact translation, but encourage them to understand the general meaning.

In addition to the suggestions in the students' book, students can sometimes compare words with similar words in their own language, or infer the meaning from the context.

Students answer the questions about *charming*.

> • *Charming* means nice, pleasant, attractive.
> • It's an adjective.
> • Similar words in the text: *delightful, attractive*

Exercise 14, page 35

Some preparation is necessary before putting students into pairs. First divide the class into A / B groups so that As work together and Bs work together in small groups. Then make sure that they understand what the symbols at the beginning of the hotel descriptions represent. Looking at the information given, students prepare the questions that they will need to ask their partners in order to find out the details of the other hotel. By preparing the questions beforehand, the A / B pairwork will be more effective and efficient. Check the questions: *What's the address? How many rooms are there? What's the price range?*, etc.

Now put the students into A / B pairs. They must not look at the other's description, but must take notes so that they have a reference when making the comparison between the two hotels. When they have shared the information, students write the comparative sentences in pairs and decide which of the two hotels they would prefer to stay or work at.

Exercise 15, page 35

Give students the following weblinks which all have lots of information about a wide range of hotels.

www.amsterdamhotelnet.com

www.1stvenicehotels.com
(This has a link to hotels in Amsterdam.)

www.hotelsvenice.com

Students should use the new vocabulary and make the hotel sound as attractive as possible without exaggerating too much. They can use the hotel descriptions in exercise 14 as a model. Half the class can find information about Amsterdam and the other half about Venice. If you prefer to make their search more specific, ask students to look for different categories of hotels so that there is variety in the information they collect. They should begin their email like this:

In reply to your enquiry, I am writing to give you information about the .... hotel in Amsterdam / Venice.

> **Extra Activity**
> 1 Students compare the emails they have written and decide which descriptions are the most attractive and why.
> 2 Students send an email to the hotel they have chosen, making enquiries. If they get a reply, compare the hotel's reply with the one the student has written.

P Photocopiable extra, see page's 2-8

Tell students that they are going to be given some information about four hotels in Amsterdam and four groups of guests. In pairs, they should talk about the hotels, compare them with each other and then choose the best hotel for each group of guests, giving reasons for their choices. When they make the comparisons they should include information such as price, range of facilities, number of rooms, suitability for families, proximity to the city centre, etc.

Now give each pair a copy of the photocopiable material and allow them time to read the information about each hotel before they begin, using the explanations of the symbols to help them interpret the information given. Tell students to use their own words and not just to read the information given.

Give a time limit, for example five minutes, and then compare answers as a class.

While the students are doing this exercise, monitor how they express themselves, paying particular attention to how they use the comparative and superlative and taking notes of their mistakes. Spend a few minutes at the end of the class focussing on any problem areas.

Consolidation 1

Unit notes

The aim of the consolidation units is to revise and consolidate the key language, functions, vocabulary and skills from the previous five units as well as to provide teachers with a diagnostic tool with which to measure progress. Exercises 1–4 revise and check the main grammar and vocabulary from the first five units. Exercises 5–8 practise the skills from these units and students practise translating from English into their mother tongue. Exercises 1–3 can be set for homework, used as a test in class or done in pairs in class.

Exercise 1, page 36

Briefly elicit the differences between the present simple and continuous before students do the exercise.

> 1 'm enjoying 2 'm meeting 3 have 4 know 5 'm not learning 6 speaks 7 'm planning 8 don't have 9 are you doing 10 Do you want

Exercise 2, page 36

Elicit the affirmative, negative and question forms of the past simple before doing the exercise.

> 1 did you do 2 went 3 did you stay 4 stayed 5 Did you do 6 met 7 saw 8 didn't have 9 had 10 You ate 11 Did you do

Exercise 3, page 37

Elicit the form and use of comparatives and superlatives before doing the exercise.

> 1 the tallest 2 the most practical 3 more exciting 4 newest 5 the latest 6 the most popular 7 the biggest 8 the most fantastic

Exercise 4, page 37

Elicit a few examples of both countable and uncountable nouns related to the world of tourism. Students explain the difference between countable and uncountable nouns and then complete both parts of the exercise in pairs.

> - countable: facility, accommodation (US), towel, sheet, bag
> - both: service
> - uncountable: tourism, information, accommodation (UK), advice, furniture, luggage, soap
>
> 1 soap, towels 2 accommodation 3 facilities 4 information 5 tourism 6 luggage, bag

Exercise 5, page 38

Ask students why someone might write a letter to a travel agency to complain about their holiday. Elicit one or two examples, e.g. *the hotel room was dirty, the service was not satisfactory*, etc. Students then work in pairs and think of as many reasons for complaining as possible. Compare ideas with the rest of the class. Turn to the letter on page 38. Students read the letter to themselves and answer the questions, underlining the appropriate information in the letter. When students give their answers, encourage them to use their own words, not just to lift the sentences from the text.

> Students should mention the following:
> - the weather
> - the view
> - the furniture
> - no TV in the room or the hotel
> - slow room service
>
> They would like their money back

Exercise 6, page 38

Before students translate the letter, ask what they have translated from English into their mother tongue before. *Do you enjoy it? Is it difficult / useful? What advice would you give to someone who wants to translate something?*

Read the tips in the professional practice box as a class and discuss why each point is important. *Why is it important to read the whole text first and not to translate each line as you read it?* Emphasise the point that the translation must sound natural in their own language even if it means changing a lot of words.

Translate the first paragraph as a class, following the tips. Students then work together in small groups and translate the rest of the letter. Compare answers and choose the best translation, explaining why one translation is better than another.

Extra Activity

An alternative way to practise translation, especially suitable for more advanced students, is for students to translate from English into their own language and then to translate back into English. Follow these steps:

• Make a photocopy of the letter and cut up into photographs. Divide the class into groups.

• Give each group one paragraph to translate into their own language. (Give the longest or most difficult paragraph to the most advanced students.) When they have finished their translations, each group exchanges their work with another group, which translates it back into English.

• Compare their translations into English with the original English text and discuss the differences and possible reasons for these differences.

Exercise 7, page 39

Look at the rainfall chart and the advert. Ask students how this information is related to the Harrisons' letter. Tell students that they are going to write a reply to the letter and should include the information in the note. Read the tips for writing letters of apology in the professional practice box. These tips will help students to write their letters, which can be done for homework. Also refer students to page 110 of the writing bank.

Exercise 8, page 39

Before students practise the dialogue in pairs, remind them that a hotel receptionist must always be polite to guests, whatever the situation and however angry or rude the guest is. Ask students about the Harrisons. *How angry are they? Do you think they will be polite to the receptionist?*

Students practise the dialogue in pairs and then act it out to the rest of the class. Each pair can act out their dialogue at the front of the class with a desk between them for the reception desk. After listening to each other's dialogue, they should also comment on how the hotel receptionists dealt with the problem. *Were they always appropriately polite? Were they apologetic enough?*

Cruise ships

Fact File

Dorling Kindersley Eyewitness Travel Guide Cruise Guide to Europe

Websites: http://travel.dk.com
　　　　 http://www.cruiseserver.net

Unit notes

Look at the picture on page 40 of the students' book and introduce the subject of cruise holidays. Students briefly describe the picture and say what it represents. Ask them what kind of people go on this type of holiday and where they go.

Exercise 1, page 40

Students discuss the advantages and disadvantages of cruise holidays and note down their ideas, before discussing them as a class. They should give reasons why they would / would not like to go on a cruise.

> • to go on holiday
> • to go on a cruise
> • Pronunciation of *cruise* /kru:z/

Exercise 2, page 40

Introduce the subject of working on a cruise ship. Ask students what kind of jobs they would expect to find and whether they would be good jobs. In pairs students look at the headings in exercise 2 before reading the magazine article and discussing possible answers. Students then scan the text to match the headings with the paragraphs in the article. Do not worry about detail yet. After checking the answers, students comment on the information in the article: *Does it sound attractive? Is it easy to get a job?*, etc.

> 1 c 2 e 3 a 4 b 5 d

Extra Activity
Students answer the questions posed by the headings, underlining the relevant information in the text and then giving their answers in their own words.

Exercise 3, page 40

Ask students what kind of people would be suitable for a job on a cruise ship. They should consider age, skills and personality and give reasons for their answers. Looking at the descriptions of the people on page 40, students then decide which of these people they think would be suitable.

> Suggested answers:
> • Teresa (sociable, loves travelling, speaks different languages, has healthcare experience, etc.)
> • Martin (has catering experience, sociable, wants a summer job)
> • Not Mario (unsociable and enjoys home life)

Exercise 4, page 41

Refer students back to the text and ask them to underline the words in exercise 4. Before students match the words with their definitions, see whether they can give their own definitions.

> 1 b 2 d 3 g 4 i 5 j 6 c 7 e 8 f 9 h 10 a

> *peak sailing periods* (paragraph 4) are the busiest periods of the year for the cruise holiday industry

Exercise 5, page 41

Students discuss the questions in pairs or small groups, giving reasons for their answers. They can talk about the advantages and disadvantages of the jobs and discuss the differences between being a waiter, entertainer, etc. on a cruise ship or on land.

Workbook homework: exercises 1 and 2, pages 24 and 25.

Exercise 6, page 42

Students describe the ship itself as well as the facilities they think are on board. Encourage students to divide the facilities into different categories, e.g. entertainment, sport, other.

Suggested answers:
- Entertainment: shows, dancing, cinema, casino, restaurants and bars
- Sport: swimming, tennis, table tennis, gym and fitness centre, sauna, jacuzzi, health centre
- Other: shops, hairdressers, doctor / medical centre

Exercise 7, page 42

Ask students to look at the pictures of the different cabins and to describe them in pairs, saying which one they would prefer to stay in. Students then label what they can before using their dictionaries.

1 drawers 2 Pullman berth 3 ladder 4 curtains
5 porthole 6 twin bed 7 balcony 8 coffee table 9 sofa
10 armchair

Exercise 8, page 42

Before putting students into A / B pairs, put them into groups of As and Bs so that they can look at their pictures together and describe them. Students look at the questions suggested on pages 114 and 116 and then decide what other questions they should ask in order to find the differences. They should all note down the questions. Now put them into A / B pairs and tell them to find the differences without looking at each other's pictures. Give them a time limit and see how many differences they find within that time, or tell them to find five differences and see which group finds them first. Discuss the differences as a class. Students decide which cabin they would prefer to have if they went on this ship.

Exercise 9, page 42

Before listening to the announcements, students look at the deck plan of the ship at the bottom of the page and talk about what people can do in the various places on board, e.g. swim, sunbathe, have a drink. Students listen and number on the deck plan the part of the ship that they hear in each announcement.

See tapescript (students' book page 135).

1 deck tennis 2 beauty rooms 3 Terrace pool 4 hair salon 5 Chaplin's Cinema 6 Al Fresco Pizzeria

Workbook homework: exercise 3, page 25.

Language focus: Present perfect

Students look at the examples and match them with the uses. Remind them that a recent event is something that has *just* happened; something that has never happened is often used with *yet*; and a life experience is usually used with *ever* in the question form.

See grammar reference section (students' book page 127).

1 c 2 b 3 a

Extra Activity

Elicit the construction of the present perfect: *have / has* + past participle. Elicit some past participles, both regular and irregular. Remind students that regular past participles are the same as the past simple and refer them to the list of irregular verbs on page 131. Set ten verbs for students to learn for homework as they did with the past simple. They should learn the infinitive, past simple and past participle so that they revise the past and learn the participle at the same time. Set ten at a time until they have learned all the verbs. Refer students back to the vocabulary recording techniques on page 21 of their students' books so that they can apply them to learning the past participles.

Exercise 10, page 43

Tell students that they are going to complete a conversation between the purser of a ship and Sarah, a new member of the crew. The purser is checking what duties Sarah has completed. All the gaps need to be filled with the present perfect and may be either positive, negative or question forms. Check answers as a class; students practise the dialogue in pairs.

The *purser* is the official on a ship responsible for the money and accounts. On a passenger ship he / she is also responsible for the comfort and welfare of passengers. There is always one purser on any kind of ship, be it a cruise liner or a military ship.

1 Have you shown 2 have you checked 3 Have you logged 4 haven't 5 have you met 6 haven't met 7 have you taken 8 've already taken 9 has Kelly shown 10 hasn't

Workbook homework: exercise 6, page 27.

Exercise 11, page 43

Before listening to the contractions, students decide where contractions can be made. They then listen, check and practise.

See tapescript (students' book page 135).

1 It's 2 They're 3 You're 4 I've 5 hasn't 6 We've
7 isn't 8 We've

Exercise 12, page 43

Students find out information about each other either by
asking *Have you ever …?* questions or by telling each
other which countries they have visited, what they have
drunk, etc., and see whether their experiences coincide.
Tell students not to worry if they cannot find an example
of each one; the important thing is to communicate with
each other. If your students have not visited other
countries, they can find examples of interesting /
important towns they have both visited in their own
country. When giving feedback to the rest of the class,
students should use the following expressions: *Both of us
have …* or *We have both …* They can also make
comments about whether they liked it or not.

Extra Activity

For more advanced students, extend the language they
should use in the pairwork.
So have I.
I haven't, but I'd really like to.
What about … , have you ever …?
You should try …, it's … .

Extra Activity

Students sometimes have problems deciding whether
to use the present perfect or the past simple as it may
be different in their own language. When the present
perfect is used to talk about experiences, there is no
reference to exactly when something happened. If
there is a time reference, the past simple is used.

Students compare these sentences:

I've **been** on a cruise ship. *(We do not know when.)*
I **went** on one **two years ago**.

Have you **ever been** to the Caribbean? *(at some time in
your life)*
Yes, I **went** there **last summer**.

Have you **been** to the pool **yet**? *(at some time today /
on your trip, etc.)*
Yes, I **went** there **this morning**.

The present perfect is also used to talk about the
period of time you have done something, e.g.

I've **been** here **for** two weeks.
I've **been** here **since** Thursday.

Workbook homework: exercises 4 and 5, page 26.

P. Photocopiable extra, see page 84

This is a mingling activity for groups of six students in
which they find out what the others have done on a cruise
ship so far.

Tell students that they are all passengers on the cruise
ship. They have only been on the ship for a few days, but
some of them have already done a lot of activities on
board. Some of them have been much lazier and have not
done much at all. They are now enjoying a cocktail party
in the Riviera bar.

Give each student a role card which tells them what they
have / have not done so far. Students ask each other
questions to find out what activities the others have done
and when they did them in order to work out who has
done the most / least.

Elicit language before starting:

A: Have you had a jacuzzi yet?
B: Oh, yes.
A: Really? When did you have one?
B: I had one this morning.

If they want to, let students expand on the dialogue and
ask more questions. To create more of a party
atmosphere, put on some background music.

At the end of the party, ask students which passengers
have done the most / least.

Exercise 13, page 44

Ask students what a CV (curriculum vitae) is and what
purpose it serves. Put students into groups and ask them
to talk about the following: *What information should be
included in a CV? In what order should the information be
presented? Why? How long should it be? Is presentation
important? What kind of style should be used?* Students are
not expected to know all the answers but by thinking
about it themselves first, they can then compare their
ideas with those of the lecturer on the CD / cassette. It
will also help them to complete the listening task.

See tapescript (students' book page 135).

A *curriculum vitae* (UK) / *résumé* (US) is a summary of one's personal, educational and professional history. The layout and content of CVs vary from country to country and often depend on the type of job applied for. In this instance a brief, simple and conventional approach that is appropriate for the job advertised has been used.

Professional practice: Writing CVs

Students read the checklist carefully before they listen and see whether they can guess any of the missing words. Students then listen and complete the gaps.

- one side
- sell, work
- at the top
- reverse
- spelling
- special abilities
interviews, best

Extra Activity

Some students may find it difficult to complete the gaps without any previous listening task. The following procedure will help them complete both exercises 13 and 14.

1 General comprehension: when students listen for the first time, ask them which of the following are mentioned:
   presentation of CV, your appearance, experience, personal details, family, qualifications, spelling, grammar, hobbies
2 True / false questions: when students listen again, ask them to state whether the following statements are true or false.

Your CV should be short.	(T)
You should 'sell' yourself.	(T)
Include all your experience.	(F)
Put your qualifications at the top of the page.	(F)
Be careful with spelling and grammar.	(T)
Qualifications are the most important thing on a CV.	(F)

Exercise 14, page 44

Bearing in mind the answers to the listening tasks, students decide in pairs how Carla can improve her CV.

Suggested answers:
- Personal details should be at the top of the page.
- Employment history should be in reverse chronological order.
- Capital letters for languages and school subjects.
- Sell yourself: *I have excellent computing skills.*
- Check spelling: qualifications, additional, details.

Fact File

GCSE (General Certificate in Secondary Education): national exit exams which schoolchildren take in Britain when finishing general secondary education at around the age of sixteen. They are usually taken by students who then proceed to higher education and then university.

GNVQ (General National Vocational Qualification): a practical / vocational qualification available to children who leave full-time schooling at sixteen. The courses are highly practical and prepare young people for higher education or employment.

Refer students to the model CV in the writing bank on page 108 of the students' book and compare the model with their improved version of the CV on page 44.

Exercise 15, page 44

Students interview each other to find out the information they require in order to write their partners' CVs. Set the written work for homework: students should write their own CV and their partner's CV so that they can compare and improve them in the next class. Students should use the model and tips in the writing bank on page 108 to help them.

Fact File

Highlight the importance of a good CV. Companies often receive numerous CVs which they sort into piles of 'accept' and 'reject'. Some people's CVs are rejected simply because of the first impression they give. If the presentation is not clean and attractive, they may be discarded straightaway. CVs should always be word processed and not written by hand or on a typewriter.

Exercise 16, page 45

Tell students what a covering letter is and why it is necessary to send one with your application and CV. Ask students what they think this letter should include. Refer them to the model covering letter in the writing bank on page 109 of the students' book and discuss what information is included (see professional practice box).

Students write their own covering letter for homework, using the model and the practice box as a reference. They should always check what kind of people the company is looking for when describing the kind of person they are. Mark their letters according to the impression they give as to the student's suitability to the job applied for.

Fact File

Covering letters: it is also important to send a good covering letter with your CV when applying for a job. It is your introduction to the company so once again the first impression is very important. Emphasise to students the importance of the presentation and content of this letter. Covering letters are always formal and brief and may be written by hand or typed.

Workbook homework: exercise 7, page 27.

Exercise 17, page 45

It is worth spending time on preparation and practice of interview simulations, as this is a crucial area for students. Job interviews can be stressful, especially the first one, so the more preparation and practice they have the better. Young people are often too casual in interviews so they need to know that it is a formal situation where first impressions are again extremely important.

Introduce the subject of interviews in general. Ask students whether they have ever had an interview for a holiday / weekend job or a school. If someone has, ask them what it was like. *How did you feel? What preparation did you make before the interview? How did it go? Did you get the job / place? What would you do differently next time?* If no one has had any experience of interviews, ask them how they would feel and what preparation they could do beforehand. Alternatively, they can ask family or friends about their experiences and share them with the rest of the class. The more exposure they have to the world of interviews the better.

Divide the class into two groups and give them their roles: A – the job applicants / B – the interviewers. Refer group A to page 116. In pairs or small groups, As prepare their questions together and Bs theirs, checking the tips carefully. Their questions should be suitable for the jobs advertised, not general.

Give them plenty of time to prepare and help them as much as necessary. Again highlight the importance of being polite and friendly. Students then practise in A / B pairs before performing for the rest of the class. If possible, set the classroom up so that it has some resemblance to an interview room, e.g. interviewer sitting opposite the interviewee.

Discuss the experience of the role-play with the class. Interviewers should say whether they would consider their applicants for the job and give their reasons why / why not. The applicants should comment on their interviewers, how they felt about being interviewed and how they could improve their performance. Students can learn a lot from each other's performance in both roles.

Extra Activity
1 Students change roles and apply for different posts with the same company.
2 In many interviews, there is more than one interviewer. Adapt the role-play so that there are two interviewers and one candidate.

To sum up the unit, discuss as a class how confident they now feel about applying for a job and being interviewed. What do they feel are the most important points to consider when applying and what problems might they face?

Service and safety

UNIT OBJECTIVES

Professional practice: writing letters of apology
Language focus: modal verbs, giving advice
Vocabulary: negative adjectives

Fact File

Dorling Kindersley Eyewitness Travel Guide South Africa

Websites: http://travel.dk.com
          www.cruiseserver.net

Unit notes

Ask students whether they know anything about South Africa and whether they think it would be a good place for a holiday.

Fact File

Despite years of political unrest and racial tension, South Africa attracts a great number of tourists from around the world all year round. The many safari parks, varied landscape, beautiful beaches, warm weather and opportunities for adventure holidays are the main attractions. The most important cities in South Africa are Cape Town, the number one tourist destination, and Johannesburg, the financial and commercial heartland of the country.

Exercise 1, page 46

Elicit jobs in hotels before looking at the pictures representing customer service. Students look at the pictures and describe the hotel staff and hotels shown. *What kind of hotels are they? How many stars might they have?* Students answer the questions in pairs.

Suggested answers:
1 receptionist (checks guests in and out of hotel)
2 porter (carries bags to rooms), room service (takes food to rooms)
3 chambermaid (cleans guestrooms)
4 doorman (watches the door, helps guests find taxis)

Exercise 2, page 46

Before they listen, ask students what information a receptionist usually asks for and gives guests when they first arrive at a hotel. They should think about what the receptionist needs to know about the guests and what the guests need to know about the hotel. When students listen for the first time they can check their ideas against the information they hear, before putting the actions in the correct order. Students listen again and this time put the actions in order and decide whether or not the receptionist is polite.

See tapescript (students' book pages 135–136).

1 d 2 c 3 f 4 a 5 g 6 h 7 e 8 b
Yes, the receptionist is polite.

Exercise 3, page 46

Look at the strategies in the professional practice box. Students discuss in pairs what they think is considered polite. Tell them that in the UK and US *please* and *thank you* are used liberally. *How much are they used in your country?*

Refer students to the tapescript for exercise 2 on pages 135–136 of the students' book. Ask them to underline any polite expressions that the receptionist uses in the dialogue.

Language focus: Modal verbs

Look at the examples and ask students whether they underlined them in the tapescript. They work out the structure from the examples. Learners often make mistakes with making polite offers, especially if the construction is very different from their own language. Give them some more examples to help: *Would you like me to call a taxi? Would you like room service to bring you some lunch?*

See grammar reference section (students' book page 128).

- *Could you* + underline{infinitive}?
- *Would you mind* + (*not*) -*ing*?
- *Do you mind* + -*ing*?
- *Would you like* + direct object + *to* + infinitive?

Pronunciation: *could* /kʊd/; *would* /wʊd/

Workbook homework: exercise 8, page 31.

Exercise 4, page 47

Students complete the questions using the language from the language focus box. Their answers may vary slightly. They then practise the dialogue in pairs.

Suggested answers:
1 Can I help you?
2 Could I have the name, please?
3 Would you like a smoking or non-smoking room?
4 Would you mind showing me your passport, please?
5 Would you like the porter to help you with your bags?

Extra Activity

Give less advanced students the missing questions and two extra ones to choose from.
Extra questions: *Could you spell your surname for me, sir? Would you like me to call your room?*

Exercise 5, page 47

Remind students of the importance of sounding polite, not just in *what* you say but also in the *way* that you say it. This exercise will help students with intonation when asking questions. Students listen to the CD / cassette and repeat each question either as a class or in turns. Some students find it difficult to hear the voice rising; to help them hear it, play the questions on the CD / cassette and ask students to look at the arrows marking the pitch in the sentences. Then repeat the sentences yourself with flat intonation and ask students whether they can hear the difference between the examples.

Exercise 6, page 47

Using the dialogue in exercise 4 as a model, students practise the procedure in pairs. More advanced students can adapt and extend the dialogue, while less advanced students can follow the dialogue making only small changes. Change roles so that everyone practises both roles. To make it more realistic, the receptionist can stand behind a desk, while the guest stands on the other side of it. Tell students to study the conversation for homework and revise it in the next class without using any model for reference or with only brief cues.

Workbook homework: exercise 7, page 31.

Exercise 7, page 48

Exercises 7 to 11 all focus on health and safety while on holiday. Check the meaning of the two words before you start. Students discuss the safety and crime in their town / city. Give them some other things to think about: *Is it more dangerous for tourists than for local people? Is it getting worse? Does it affect tourism? Will it affect tourism in the future? Is anything being done about it? What can be done about it?*

Exercise 8, page 48

Before playing the CD / cassette, ask students whether they know anything about crime and public safety in South Africa. If not, go straight on to the listening exercise. When they listen for the first time, ask students just to listen and to decide whether Cape Town sounds like a dangerous city. (Yes, it does.) *How does it compare to your town / city?* Students read the questions carefully before listening again and completing the answers. Check answers and ask whether they would like to go to Cape Town on holiday.

See tapescript (students' book page 136).

1 go shopping in the city centre
2 large amounts of cash
3 in the safe deposit box in their room
4 keep doors locked at all times
5 the poorer areas of the city
6 Robben Island

Fact File

Robben Island is situated eleven kilometres from Cape Town, in the middle of Table Bay, within sight of the city. It was on this island that Nelson Mandela was held prisoner for eighteen years. Before being a prison for political activists during the Apartheid era, the island was a leper colony. The island is now a museum and conservation area and was declared a World Heritage site in 1999. Nowadays it is a popular tourist attraction.

Exercise 9, page 48

The vocabulary in this exercise comes from the conversation at the Cape Grace Hotel. Students can either use dictionaries or work out the answers by guessing the meanings of the words through context. Students can find the words in the tapescript on page 136 of the students' book.

1 b **2** f **3** d **4** c **5** a **6** e

Check the pronunciation of *jewellery* /ˈdʒuːəlri/. This is not an easy word to pronounce so help students to pronounce it correctly by asking them to repeat after you or to listen to it on the CD / cassette and repeat.

Language focus: Giving safety advice

These phrases are also taken from the conversation at the Cape Grace Hotel. Either ask students to read the phrases and find them in the tapescript on page 136 or to look at the tapescript and underline examples of useful phrases for giving advice. They can then check their examples with those in the language focus box. Students practise the phrases in pairs, giving each other advice about being careful in their town / city. These phrases will be practised further in exercises 11 and 12.

See grammar reference section (students' book page 128).

Workbook homework: exercises 1, 2 and 3, pages 28–29.

Exercise 10, page 48

Ask students what they know about safaris. *Would you like to go on safari? Is it dangerous? What preparations would you have to make before you went?* Students look at the pictures on page 49 and describe them in pairs. Does it look attractive? Students look at exercise 10 and match the words with their definitions using dictionaries.

1 b 2 f 3 e 4 a 5 g 6 d 7 h 8 c

Exercise 11, page 49

This speaking exercise needs some preparation before doing the pairwork. Before looking at the text, ask students to predict in pairs what people can and cannot do on a safari. Students should then scan the text and check their ideas against what is written in the text.

Divide the class into two groups: visitors (A) and hotel receptionists (B). Group A reads the text and underlines the information they would like to ask the receptionist. Then they prepare questions to obtain this information by putting the 'giving advice phrases' on page 48 into question form. Give them some examples: *Where is the best place to see wildlife? Can we get out of the car?*

Group B also reads the text, underlines the important information and writes the advice using the same phrases. Give them some examples: *You mustn't / shouldn't drive fast. You mustn't leave your car, except at the picnic areas.*

Encourage students to use as many different expressions for asking for / giving advice as they can. Students practise the dialogue in A / B pairs. The guest can also ask follow-up questions, e.g. *Why mustn't we leave our cars?* Students can refer to their books during the pairwork, but should try to use their own words as much as possible, rather than just reading straight from the text.

Suggested questions:
- Is it best to drive slowly?
- Can we feed the animals?
- What do you recommend we do if we want a cigarette?
- What's the best way to protect ourselves from the sun?
- How can we avoid snakes?
- Is it a good idea to take malaria pills?

Suggested answers:
- You must drive slowly.
- You shouldn't give food to the animals.
- You mustn't throw away burning matches or cigarettes.
- I recommend you wear a hat and sunblock.
- It's a good idea to watch where you put your hands and feet.
- It's best to take precautions against malaria.

Exercise 12, page 49

Set this webtask for homework. They can find information from the search engines www.google.com and www.ask.co.uk by typing in 'health and safety advice for tourists in (*name of their city / country*)'. They should make notes on the information they find and be prepared to discuss it in groups in the next class. Students can use their own knowledge as well as the information they find on the internet.

Travel guide project

Personal security and health
Students write a tourist advice page to add to their projects, including any advice they think is useful and using the 'giving advice phrases'. They can illustrate it with their own pictures, pictures from the internet or from information they find at the local tourist information centre.

Workbook homework: exercise 5, page 30.

Exercise 13, page 50

Students work in pairs, and answer the following questions:

What do you think a guest satisfaction questionnaire is?

What might the hotel ask about? (Staff, rooms, excursions, etc.)

What might guests say / complain about? (Dirty rooms, rude waiters, etc.)

Why do hotels use them? (To find out guests' opinions about the service they have received and thus improve it where necessary.)

Students look at the quotes and compare them with the complaints they suggested. *Do you think these are serious complaints? Which one do you think is the most serious? What should the hotel do about them?*

Now look at the questionnaire and discuss its contents and the comments of the guest. *Does the questionnaire cover every aspect of the accommodation and service? How satisfied / dissatisfied is the guest? What will / can the hotel do about it?* Students now match the quotes above with the comments in the questionnaire.

1 d **2** c **3** a **4** b **5** f **6** e

Workbook homework: exercise 4, page 29.

Exercise 14, page 51

Tell students that they are going to hear four different members of staff giving their responses to the comments in the questionnaire. Ask students to imagine what they might say. When they listen for the first time, students decide who is speaking. If necessary, give them the jobs of the four people and ask them to put them in order of speaking: *entertainment rep, porter, waiter, receptionist.* The second time they listen, they make notes of what their reasons are.

See tapescript (students' book page 136).

1 porter; he was very busy
2 receptionist; she was acting as a guide although it is not her job
3 entertainment rep; the information was out of date
4 waiter; the guest changed his mind and the waiter was busy

With the information they have, students match the explanations with the action that Paula needs to take.

1 a **2** d **3** b **4** c

Exercise 15, page 51

Ask students what they think Paula will / should do about the dissatisfied guest. *How can she improve the situation with him / her? What would you do in her situation?* Read the note for Paula on page 50 and compare the instructions with their ideas. Make sure students understand *a letter of apology. What will she mention in the letter? Is the free night a good solution?*

Refer students to the expressions for a letter of apology. Check that they understand the expressions before completing the letter. When the letter is completed, look at the tip box with the guidelines on replying to a complaint and match them with the contents of the letter. This will help students understand the structure of the genre when they write their own letters of apology.

1 We were very sorry to hear
2 Unfortunately
3 we need to improve
4 Please find enclosed
5 We would like to offer you
6 we apologise for any inconvenience

Workbook homework: exercise 6, page 30.

Extra Activity
To conclude the unit, ask students whether they would feel confident about dealing with customer complaints. *What do they think is the best way to deal with dissatisfied customers? What solutions are there?*

8 East meets West

Fact File

Dorling Kindersley Eyewitness Travel Guide Istanbul
Websites: http://travel.dk.com, www.turkey.org

Unit notes

Fact File

Istanbul, which was the capital of Turkey until 1923, is unusual in its location in that it spreads over two continents: half of the city is in Europe while the other half is in Asia. The city is divided by the Golden Horn which is an inlet of the Bosphorus that forms a large natural harbour. Istanbul is the country's largest and most visited city, being the location of famous sites such as the Grand Bazaar, the Blue Mosque and Hagia Sophia (an impressive Byzantine church).

Exercise 1, page 52

Let students look at and discuss the pictures on page 52–53 of the students' book. Elicit the types of tourism shown on these pages.

- Bridge over the Bosphorus, dividing the bustling city of Istanbul.
- Ancient architecture of the Roman Theatre at Ephesus and the Castle of St Peter.
- The natural mineral pools at Pamukkale.

Exercise 2, page 52

Tell students that they are going to hear part of a radio programme in which people talk about their holidays. They should listen to where the people like to go on holiday and why. If you think that students will have problems understanding the names of the destinations, write them on the board and let them choose the appropriate answers. Add some extra destinations to make it more challenging.

See tapescript (students' book page 136).

Before listening, students will need to know the following useful words:
A *resort* is a place where people go on holiday such as a *seaside*, *mountain* or *ski resort*.
A *hot spot* is a place that is extremely popular.

1 Corfu; something for all the family
2 Majorca; sun, sea and sangría
3 Turkey; great sightseeing

Exercise 3, page 52

Students read the true / false questions carefully before listening to the next part of the programme. When they listen for the first time, they should answer just *true* or *false*. When listening again, students check answers and make notes to correct the false statements.

See tapescript (students' book pages 136–137).

crowded: too full of people
leaflet: a small piece of printed paper giving information or advertising something

1 F (Turkish beaches aren't as crowded as beaches in, say, Spain.)
2 F (There are other smaller places that are more interesting.)
3 F ('Cotton Castle')
4 T
5 T
6 F (It has a website.)

Workbook homework: exercises 1 and 2, page 32.

Exercise 4, page 53

Before students mark the connected words, they need a brief explanation of what connected speech is (see below). The examples will help them when they do the exercise. Play the sentences a number of times as students may find it difficult to hear the connections at first. Students practise saying the sentences once the answers have been checked.

See tapescript (students' book page 137).

Connected speech. Tell students that we normally speak by producing a connected stream of sounds rather than individual separated words. Two features of connected speech are:
a) when the end of one word runs into the next, e.g. *Good afternoon*.
b) some letters at the end of a word are not pronounced at all and flow into the following word, e.g. *Wha(t) do you do?*

> 1 Goo(d) morning an(d) welcome to Holiday Options.
> 2 Oh, it's go(t) to be Majorca. I love it.
> 3 I've been to Majorca twice now.
> 4 Do you think Turkey'll be popular this year?
> 5 An(d) do you think Turkey migh(t) be a hot spot?

Workbook homework: exercise 8, page 35.

Exercise 5, page 53

Before dividing students into pairs, ask them to compare a few resorts in their country, in order to elicit and revise comparative and superlative forms. Write some examples on the board so that students can use them as a reference when they are comparing resorts in pairs. This exercise can be done just as a speaking exercise or extended to a written exercise to include in their projects (see below). When each pair has chosen their three resorts, join pairs to make groups of four to compare their ideas. The members of each group should agree amongst them which are the three most popular resorts, giving their reasons according to the same points mentioned in the box. Depending on the size of the group and the time available, expand the groups further. Again the new groups agree on the three most popular resorts. Continue in the same way and see whether the whole class can reach a consensus.

Language focus: Predictions and intentions

Tell students that there are various ways to talk about future predictions and intentions. Ask them to read the information in the language box and to answer the following questions, making their own brief notes. These questions will help them focus on the important points and give them a reason for reading the information. *How many different ways can we express predictions and intentions? What are they? When do we use each one?* Ask students to write their own example of each one. Tell them that *will* and *going to* are often interchangeable, depending on how the situation is interpreted.

See grammar reference section (students' book page 128).

Exercise 6, page 54

Students write their answers, using the information in the language box to help. Students should then compare their answers with a partner's and give reasons for their choice. Many of the answers are interchangeable.

> 1 is going to be
> 2 will / is going to replace
> 3 will / are going to be
> 4 will / are going to be
> 5 won't / isn't going to be
> 6 will / is going to be
> 7 won't / aren't going to stay, will probably go
> 8 will probably keep

Workbook homework: exercises 4, 5 and 6, pages 34 and 35.

Exercise 7, page 55

Before looking at the gifts and souvenirs from Istanbul, ask students: *Do you like to buy souvenirs when they go somewhere new? What kind of things do you like to buy? Who do you buy them for? What do you usually buy for yourself?* In pairs, students describe the pictures and read the information about the gifts. They decide what they would / would not like for themselves. Then they decide what they would buy for each person and why.

Fact File

bazaar: a market or group of shops, especially in the Middle East or India
handicrafts: objects made by hand

Workbook homework: exercise 3, page 33.

Exercise 8, page 55

Before talking about traditional gifts from other countries, ask students about typical souvenirs from their own country. *What do tourists usually buy when they come? Are they useful gifts? What would you recommend a visitor to buy?*

The webtask can be set for homework; students share the information they have found with each other in the next class. They should be able to describe the gifts, saying what they are used for and of course where they can be bought. If possible they should find pictures of the gifts to show each other.

Travel guide project

What to buy in your country
Students write descriptions of typical gifts from their country in their projects. They should say who they are suitable for, whether they are expensive and what they are used for. They can add photos or drawings to illustrate the gifts.

Exercise 9, page 55

Elicit from students which tense they need to use when talking about holiday plans. If they know for sure, use *going to*; if not, use *I'm not sure, but I think I'll* …or *I may / might* … . Check question forms so that they ask each other questions to find out about their partner's plans using the prompts in the box. Ask them which holiday sounds better: theirs or their partner's? Why?

Exercise 10, page 56

Before focussing on the listening task, ask students about the tourist industry in their country. *Is it on the increase? Are there more tourists now than before? What kind of tourists are they? Do you think that the type of tourism is changing?*

Read the instructions for the listening exercise and ask students what they understand by *a new type of tourist* and *changes in the type of holidays*. In small groups, students discuss the four subjects and predict what they think the experts will say about each subject. Students listen and match, giving reasons for their choices. Tell them that they only need to listen for the gist of each extract.

See tapescript (students' book page 137).

1 b **2** c **3** d **4** a

Exercise 11, page 56

Students look at the statements and decide whether they are true or false before listening again. They do not need to remember what the speakers said as they can give their own ideas too. Listen and check their answers according to what the speakers say. *Are they surprised by any of the information?* Ask students to think of any other changes there might be in the travel industry in the future.

1 T
2 F (people will take fewer long holidays and more short breaks)
3 F (costs will continue to come down)
4 F (Russia, China, India, Indonesia and Thailand)
5 F (the majority will continue to buy package holidays)

P. Photocopiable extra, see page 85

Divide students into pairs or groups of three and give each pair / group a copy of the board game, counters and a dice.

Students take it in turns to throw the dice. When they land on a square with a prediction on it, they must talk for thirty seconds about whether they agree or disagree with the statement and explain why. The other students in the group keep track of the time. If the student cannot speak for as long as thirty seconds he / she must go back to the square he / she came from. The winner is the first player to arrive at the last square.

While students are doing this activity, monitor them and make a note of their mistakes. Spend some time at the end of the game correcting the mistakes.

Exercise 12, page 56

Tell students that when learning new words, it is useful to learn synonyms or similar meanings and antonyms or opposite meanings. Students match the opposites, most of which are from the listening extracts. In pairs, referring back to what the experts said and using their own ideas, students practise the vocabulary by writing sentences about the future of the tourist industry.

1 b **2** d **3** e (*less* + uncountable; *fewer* + countable) **4** f **5** a **6** c

Exercise 13, page 56

Introduce the theme of the tourist industry exploiting and spoiling beautiful locations. Ask students why this happens and what they think about it. *Do you know anywhere that has been spoilt by tourism?* Tell students to look at the map and to describe it in pairs. They should also discuss the advantages and disadvantages of developing an island like this.

Students read the instructions for exercise 13 and discuss the questions in pairs before listening. They predict the answers to the questions and share ideas with the rest of the class. Students listen and complete the answers. After checking the answers, discuss the proposal for the island as a class. *What do you think of the proposal? What effect would it have on the island and the islanders? Are there more advantages or disadvantages? Should the proposal be accepted? Why / why not?*

See tapescript (students' book pages 137–138).

Students mark on map:
- airport south of Bellavista
- resort north of monuments
- car park and visitors' centre near stones

1 By ferry or plane.
2 To the north of ancient monuments.
3 A museum, a shop, a restaurant and a café.
4 Two hotels and a camp site, local rooms.
5 It will improve the island's economy and make Hermosa famous.

Extra Activity

To simplify the questions in the listening exercise, give students different options for each question. Students circle the correct answer(s). Tell them that some questions have more than one example in the answer:
1 by boat / ferry / helicopter / plane
2 near the fishing port / the delta / the ancient monuments
3 swimming pool / museum / shop / children's play area / restaurant / café
4 hotels / youth hostel / bed and breakfast / camp site / local rooms
5 to improve the island's economy / to make Hermosa more beautiful / to make Hermosa famous

Professional practice: Giving presentations

Tell students that they are going to learn how to give simple presentations, which is a very important skill for people working in the tourism industry. Presentations need to be well organised and well delivered in order to be effective. Students look at the tapescript on pages 137–138, underline the useful language and complete the sentences with the appropriate expressions. Tell students that in addition to organising presentations well and using the appropriate language, you need to sound confident and convincing. Students practise saying the phrases, using the CD / cassette again if necessary. The phrases and the model presentation in the tapescript will help students in exercise 14.

- Today I'm going to talk about …
- First of all, I'd like to talk about …
- Then I'll talk about …
- Finally, I'll talk about …
- The main advantage of this is that …
- To sum up …

Workbook homework: exercise 7, page 35.

Exercise 14, page 57

Look at the map of the island again and focus on the three possible sites for development. Give each group one of the sites, otherwise they might all choose the same one. If possible let two groups work on each site so that the other groups can then discuss which proposal is better and vote for the best one. Give students enough time to prepare their presentations in their groups. Each group chooses someone to present their proposal.

Extra Activity

Record students giving their presentations on cassette or, if you have access to a video camera, record them on video. The recordings can be used to help them improve their delivery and pronunciation. The task can be repeated at the end of the course and compared with the original recording.

tourist board: an organisation in charge of making rules about the tourist industry and marketing the area to encourage tourism

(9) Window seat or aisle?

Fact File

Websites: http://travel.dk.com
www.britishairways.com

Unit notes

Introduce the theme of air travel by asking students whether they have ever flown. In groups students share their experiences of air travel. Give them some prompts if necessary: *Where did you go? Did you enjoy the flight? Were you nervous?* For those who have never travelled by plane, ask them whether they would like to fly. *Where would you like to go? What do you think it would be like?*

Exercise 1, page 58

In pairs, students decide the names of the different jobs and what the people are doing. *Can you think of other jobs that people do at airports?* Discuss which jobs they would / would not like to do.

1 flight attendant; serving drinks to passengers
2 check-in agent; checking passengers in to a flight
3 flight attendant; helping passengers to stow their bags safely

Exercise 2, page 58

Ask students who have travelled by plane about the check-in procedure. *What happened and what questions were you asked? How long did it take? What luggage did you have? What did you take onto the plane with you?* Students look at the pictures on page 58, identify what they represent and then match the pictures with the procedures outlined on the webpage on page 59.

1 f 2 h 3 d 4 b 5 g 6 c 7 e 8 a

Pronunciation: change of stress
check-in (n); *to check in* (v)

Exercise 3, page 58

Students look at the statements in pairs and, before reading the webpage again, decide whether they are true or false, giving reasons for their choice. Encourage students to underline the relevant information in the text.

1 T 2 F (every piece of luggage must be labelled)
3 T 4 F (only unidentified objects) 5 T 6 F (do not carry replica weapons) 7 F (it is recommended, but is not an obligation) 8 T

Fact File

Air travel changed in many ways after the terrorist attack on the World Trade Center on 11 September 2001. The check-in procedure became longer and stricter on long-haul flights and the number of items of cabin luggage considered as a security risk increased. Now you cannot take sharp objects of any kind, including nail scissors, penknives, plastic toy weapons, etc.

Workbook homework: exercises 1 and 2, pages 36–37.

Exercise 4, page 59

Tell students to cover up the definitions and to look at the words in the left-hand column associated with check-in. In pairs, students explain the meaning of each word before matching with the definitions. They may use dictionaries if necessary. Check the answers with the whole class. In order to learn the vocabulary, students then work in pairs with only one of them looking at the words and the definitions. Student A gives either the word or the definition and B supplies the missing definition or word. Alternatively this exercise can be set for homework and checked in pairwork as described above. Tell students they will need this vocabulary in exercise 6.

1 b 2 d 3 h 4 f 5 a 6 c 7 e 8 g

Workbook homework: exercise 3, page 37.

Exercise 5, page 59

More advanced students can prepare the dialogue directly in A / B pairs. With less advanced students, divide the class into an A and a B group. Group A students turn to page 117 and prepare their questions together while group B students prepare some questions that they can ask the check-in attendant. Students then divide into A / B pairs and practise the dialogues with their questions already prepared.

Language focus: Modal verbs of obligation

Look at the 'degrees of obligation line' together. Students sometimes have difficulty in interpreting grammar lines, so make sure that they understand what it represents. The explanation for each modal verb below the line will help them to understand what it means if they cannot work it out from the diagram.

See grammar reference section (students' book page 129).

Extra Activity

To make sure that students read the grammar explanation carefully, give them the following questions:
- *Which modal verb(s) do you use when something is not necessary?* (don't have to)
- *Which do you use for strong obligation?* (must / mustn't / have to)
- *Which do you use as advice or recommendation?* (should / shouldn't)

You may wish to give them a list of modal verbs to choose from. Students answer the questions and make their own notes.

• Highlight that *don't have to* does not mean the opposite of *have to*.
• Pronunciation of *mustn't* /ˈmʌsənt/

Exercise 6, page 60

In pairs, students look at the symbols and interpret what they represent, using either English or their own language. Check their interpretations to make sure that they all have the right idea. Either ask students to match the symbols with the regulations given or ask them to write their own regulations for each symbol before looking at the examples below. This alternative exercise gives students the opportunity to decide which modal verb is appropriate in each case and to think about how to express the regulations in their own words. They can then compare their examples with the ones in the students' book.

1 b 2 d 3 g 4 h 5 c 6 e 7 f 8 a

Workbook homework: exercises 4 and 6, page 38.

Exercise 7, page 61

Tell students that they are going to do a pairwork exercise between a flight attendant and a passenger on a plane. The flight attendant will answer the passenger's questions using appropriate modal verbs of obligation.

Put students into pairs. A is a flight attendant, B is a passenger. Student A looks at the information on page 61 and B looks at the questions on page 118. Give them time to look at their respective information and to ask any questions if necessary. Remind students that they should both be polite. The passengers should begin with *Excuse me, please*…, and use *please* and *thank you* where necessary. Flight attendants should address the passengers as *Sir* or *Madam*.

Students ask and answer the questions. Go around the class and monitor the pairs. Check the answers as a class. If you think it necessary, students can write up the questions and answers after the speaking exercise or for homework.

• *crew*: all the people working on a plane, ship, etc.
• *cabin crew*: people taking care of the passengers on a plane

Exercise 8, page 61

Before answering the questions, students look at the information screen and comment on the information that is there. Ask them the following questions. *What do the letters represent?* (Abbreviations of airports and airlines.) *Why is the information written in this way?* (To save space.) Students look at the information and answer the questions.

• *boarding*: passengers can go onto the plane
• *delayed*: the flight is late
• *cancelled*: the flight is not going

.1 EWR 2 LHR 3 OP BY 4 three 5 You arrive at that time on the following day.

Tell students that they are going to hear various airport announcements. Ask them what information they expect to hear. Students listen and complete the missing information. The information is in order but there are some extra announcements.

See tapescript (students' book page 138).

> **1** BA184 **2** 43 **3** BOARDING **4** UA906
> **5** CANCELLED **6** 38 **7** DELAYED

Workbook homework: exercise 5, page 38.

Exercise 9, page 61

Ask students what information they like to know before they go to a new place. *Where do you find this information? Is it necessary to know a lot about a place before you get there?* Briefly ask what advice or information would be useful for someone visiting their town / country. *What do visitors definitely need to know before they come?* If necessary brainstorm some categories for students to discuss, e.g. safety, things to bring, clothes to wear, places to avoid, etc.

Give students enough time to discuss the advice and information that they think is necessary, following the points given. When writing their leaflets, they should use a variety of modal verbs of obligation. Compare the leaflets, including the information and the presentation. *How can they be improved?*

> **Extra Activity**
> 1 Extend the exercise by asking students to find information on the internet or from the local tourist board which they can adapt for their leaflet. *Does the tourist office have a special advice / information leaflet?* Students bring the information they find to class and share it with their group before preparing their leaflet.
> 2 This writing exercise can be added to their travel guide projects.

Exercise 10, page 62

Before listening to David Torra, ask students about the training of cabin crew. *What do you think they have to learn? Do you think the training is easy? What skills and personal qualities do cabin crew need to have?* Ask students to look at the different parts of the training process and to discuss in pairs how difficult they think each part is and what it might involve. They then listen and tick when each part happens.

See tapescript (students' book page 138).

> Weeks 1 & 2: read an airline ticket, different types of aircraft, collect new uniform
> Weeks 3 & 4: safety and emergency procedures, emergency flight simulations, medical training
> Week 5: how to serve food and drink, first real flight

> *simulation*: an activity or situation that produces conditions which are not real but have the appearance of being real, used especially to test something

Exercise 11, page 62

Before listening again, students read the questions carefully, answering some of them if they can remember the information from the previous listening. When the answers have been checked, students comment on the training course in pairs: *Does the training prepare cabin crew for every event? Do you think that you would be ready for the real job after the course? What do you think is the most difficult part of the training / job?*

> *mock* (adj): pretend
> *probation period*: a length of time, during which someone who has just started a job is tested to see whether they are suitable for what they are doing: *My contract has a three-month probation period.*

> **1** life jackets, fire extinguishers
> **2** a simulated plane where the cabin crew do their training
> **3** part of the group of trainees
> **4** emergency landing, fire
> **5** by playing the sounds of people screaming and the engines running
> **6** burns, birth
> **7** cook and serve meals, make drinks and set up the drinks trolley
> **8** six months

> **Extra Activity**
> If you think that the comprehension questions are too difficult, ask true / false questions:
> 1 *David talks about life jackets and fire extinguishers.*   (T)
> 2 *A 'mockab' is a simulated plane where the training takes place.*   (T)
> 3 *Regular plane travellers are invited to act as passengers.*   (F)
> 4 *David talks about practising emergencies.*   (T)
> 5 *The trainers scream and run engines to simulate an emergency.*   (F)
> 6 *David refers to the birth of a baby and burns as examples of medical emergencies.*   (T)
> 7 *In the final week the trainees learn how to cook and serve meals.*   (T)
> 8 *The probation period is three months.*   (F)

Exercise 12, page 63

Check that students know the meaning of *duty-free* and ask them for examples of goods that can be bought duty-free. Ask where you can buy duty-free goods: at an airport, port, on a plane, on a ferry. Students listen and complete the answers.

It is a good idea if students read the tapescript on pages 138–139 of the students' book in pairs as this will help them with the pairwork in exercise 13.

> *cuddly toy*: a soft toy for children to *cuddle* (hold in their arms), e.g. a teddy bear, monkey, cat, etc.

1 fifty millilitres **2** $43.30 **3** leopard, teddy bear
4 teddy bear **5** $57.90

Workbook homework: exercises 7 and 8, page 39.

> Different ways of saying prices in dollars:
> *Fifty dollars and twenty-five cents.*
> *Fifty dollars twenty-five.*
> *Fifty twenty-five.*
> Pounds and Euros can be expressed in the same way.

P Photocopiable extra, see page 86

In this exercise, students practise making appropriate comments in response to various situations that are described on the cards in the photocopiable section of this book.

Divide the class into small groups and give each group a copy of the situations on page 86, cut up into separate cards. Students read the situations one by one and decide together what they would / should say in reply to each one. Alternatively, students take it in turns to read a situation card to themselves. They then give a suitable reply and the other people in the group have to guess what the situation is. The person who guesses the situation keeps the card. Count up the number of cards each person has at the end to see who is the winner.

Choose one card to demonstrate before the students do the exercise in their groups.

(10) Business or pleasure?

Fact File

Dorling Kindersley Eyewitness Travel Guide Cracow

Websites: http://travel.dk.com
www.explore-krakow.com

Unit notes

Introduce the unit by asking students to think of reasons why people travel. *Do you know anyone who travels regularly? What is their reason for travelling?*

Exercise 1, page 64

Students look at the pictures, describe the travellers in each picture and state their reasons for travelling.

1 going to sports event 2 family holiday 3 business
Other reasons for travelling: to learn a new language, experience new cultures, see friends and relations, go to music festivals, investigate family history, go on a pilgrimage, etc.

Exercise 2, page 64

Students continue working in pairs and discuss the needs of each type of traveller in the pictures. Compare answers as a class.

Suggested answers:
Business travellers
- Transport: comfortable, fast – time and schedule is more important than cost, e.g. scheduled, business-class flights
- Accommodation: comfortable and suitable for work with business facilities, meeting rooms, internet connection, etc., reasonably priced, e.g. business rates for companies
- Catering: sophisticated, suitable for entertaining business clients
- Entertainment: shows / dinners

Sports fans
- Transport: cheap and direct to sports venue, e.g. coach
- Accommodation: convenient, budget accommodation suitable for groups
- Catering: inexpensive snacks and bar meals
- Entertainment: nightlife such as pubs and clubs

Families
- Transport: easy and convenient, reasonably priced, e.g. economy class when flying
- Accommodation: comfortable but not luxurious, convenient, i.e. not far from shops or the beach
- Catering: self-catering, cheap, food that is suitable for children
- Entertainment: cheap, family entertainment, e.g. leisure centre, children's activities, etc.

Exercise 3, page 64

Students discuss the questions in pairs, giving reasons for their answers. Answers may vary. Extend the exercise by asking the following questions: *Do they know anyone who travels for business reasons? Do they enjoy it? Would they like a job that involved a lot of travel?* In pairs, students talk about the advantages and disavantages of business travelling.

Suggested answers:
1 businessperson
2 scheduled
3 three, four or five star
4 plane, taxi, train
5 They travel frequently and are sometimes in large groups, e.g. for conferences, trade fairs, etc. Business travel is a large source of income as companies are often prepared to spend money on top hotels, restaurants and extras such as room service.

Fact File

scheduled flight: a plane service that flies at the same time every day, every week. These flights can be expensive but are very reliable in general.
charter flight: a low-cost journey on a plane on which all the places have been paid for in advance by travel companies for their customers. These flights are often subject to delays.

Exercise 4, page 64

Students look at the symbols and interpret what they represent, explaining them in their own words. Make sure that they know the meaning of *facilities* (i.e. the services that are provided for a particular purpose at a hotel, leisure centre, etc.). They may need the help of a dictionary for some of the facilities.

1 a fax connection 2 gym / fitness facilities 3 air-conditioning 4 TV in room 5 24-hour room service 6 access for wheelchairs 7 business facilities 8 suitable for children 9 credit cards accepted 10 conference facilities

Suggested answers:
1, 3, 5, 7, 9, 10 (perhaps also 2, 4)

Other important facilities:
- Location: near trade fair / conference / the company's offices. Easy access to airport.
- Comfort: the hotel should be comfortable, relaxing and quiet for work purposes.
- Time saving: express check-in / check-out.

Workbook homework: exercise 3, page 41.

Exercise 5, page 65

The text from the webpage is a detailed description of the facilities at the Forum Hotel.

When students read the text for the first time, ask them to read for gist and to answer the following questions: *Why is this hotel suitable for business travellers? Is it suitable for other types of travellers too?* This will help them to get a general idea before they start reading in more detail.

Students read the text again and choose the appropriate titles for each paragraph.

Extra Activity
As an alternative reading exercise, ask students to read the text without reading the titles and to decide the contents of each paragraph. They choose their own titles and then compare them with the ones given.

1 Location 2 Dining 3 Accommodation 4 Leisure 5 Facilities 6 Meeting facilities

Exercise 6, page 65

Students find the italicised words in the text and explain in pairs what each word / expression means. If they do not know the meaning of some words, encourage them to guess the meaning from the context. Students complete the sentences.

1 equipped with 2 rooftop 3 offers 4 full range 5 able to accommodate 6 dishes 7 indoor, outdoor 8 at our guests' disposal

Workbook homework: exercises 1 and 2, pages 40–41.

Exercise 7, page 66

In pairs, students describe the places in the pictures, saying which places look interesting and what they could do in each one. Students tell their partners which three places they would most like to visit. Ask students these extra questions to find out what they think of Cracow in general: *Does Cracow look like a good place to go on holiday? What kind of people would enjoy going there?*

Exercise 8, page 66

Tell students that they are going to hear a conversation between a hotel receptionist and a guest. The guest would like to go sightseeing in Cracow and asks the receptionist for information about the city.

When they listen for the first time, students look at the pictures in exercise 7 and tick the places that the receptionist recommends.

See tapescript (students' book page 139).

1 the market square 2 disco

Exercise 9, page 66

Students read the questions carefully before listening again and predict some of the answers if possible. Prediction is a useful skill when doing listening tasks: even if students do not predict the right answer, they have given some thought to it and have an idea about what kind of answer might be given. Sometimes answers can be predicted by using one's common sense.

Help students with this technique. Look at question 1 and brainstorm reasons why Laura might have little free time for sightseeing, e.g. *She is there for a very short time. She is very busy doing other things,* etc.

Students listen and answer the questions.

1 She's attending a conference and is flying back to the UK on Sunday night.
2 About three hours / a whole morning.
3 There are long queues.
4 A cellar bar with cabaret and disco.
5 She does not want to go dancing.
6 To go to the pub *U Louisa*.

Exercise 10, page 66

Students look at the tapescript on page 139. Tell them that there are seven expressions in the text. Students underline the expressions and once checked, write them out in their notes so that they have a good reference whenever they need to use them. Focus their attention on when to use -ing or the infinitive and which expressions are followed by a noun.

- *How about visiting* the Wawel Castle?
- … *it's worth* a visit.
- *You must see* the dragon's cave.
- *You should get* there early.
- *Why don't you go* to Pod Baranami?
- *What about* jazz?
- *You could go* to the pub, U Louisa.

Language focus: Modal verbs: *can, could* and *might*

Look at the explanations and examples, focussing on form and function. Students add these expressions to their list of suggestions and recommendations. They will need to refer to them in exercise 12.

See grammar reference section, page 129.

Workbook homework: exercises 4 and 5, page 42.

Exercise 11, page 67

Students look at the pictures of Wawel Hill and read the descriptions. They then describe the pictures in pairs. Ask students whether they like castles and whether they would like to visit this one. *Why / why not?* Students check the names of the items in the pictures in their dictionaries.

Pronunciation of objects in pictures:
castle /ˈkɑːsəl/
cloak /kləʊk/
tomb /tuːm/
statue /ˈstætʃuː/
dragon /ˈdrægən/

Ask students whether they are interested in history. *When you go on holiday do you like to visit historic places? Or do you find them boring? Are you interested in the history of where you live? Do you know much about it?*

Students read the events, dates and periods carefully before listening to the CD / cassette. Focus their attention on the way dates and periods are expressed and the prepositions that are used with them. Students listen to the tour on the CD / cassette and match the events with the dates.

1 c 2 e 3 d 4 b 5 a
The group is standing in front of the statue of Tadeusz Kościuszko.

Extra Activity

The Public Holidays box shows all the public holidays in Poland. You can use this box for discussion of public holidays and to review the expression of dates. Students discuss the public holidays in Poland and compare them with public holidays in their country. *Which country has more holidays? Which ones are the same? Which are different? Do you have any that they do not have in Poland?*

Remind students that dates are written in one way and said in another. Elicit how dates can be said in English:
The first of June
June the first
June first (US)

Workbook homework: exercise 6, page 43.

Exercise 12, page 67

Before setting up the pairs, elicit expressions for making suggestions and recommendations from exercise 10. Put the expressions on the board so that students can refer to them if necessary. Tell them that they are going to do a role-play between a hotel receptionist and a guest who wants some advice about what do in Cracow at night.

The pairs practise the dialogue and student B decides which recommendations to follow. Ask B students whether they like the recommendations. Ask the class whether they think Cracow has good nightlife. Find out what students like to do at night when they are on holiday. *Can you recommend anywhere with good nightlife? Does your town have good nightlife for tourists?*

Extra Activity

If necessary, less advanced students can refer back to the tapescript on page 139 when practising the dialogue.

Travel guide project

Your town by night
Students write suggestions and recommendations for going out at night in their town / country, using a variety of expressions. They can also include information about dress code, age restrictions and warnings if there are any places that tourists should avoid at night.

Exercise 13, page 68

Students look at the floor plans of the conference rooms and compare them in pairs. They decide which plan is more suitable for business conferences and give reasons for their choice. Students then scan the fax to find out which floor plan is described. Tell students not to focus on other details yet.

> 2

> * *banqueting room*: a room for a formal dinner, usually large
> * *boardroom*: a room where directors of a company have meetings

Exercise 14, page 69

Elicit what equipment is necessary for conferences. Look at the pictures and describe the function of each piece of equipment in pairs. Students then look back at the fax and match the pictures with the equipment mentioned in the fax. Read the following paragraph which mentions the support services, i.e. extra services. In pairs, students answer the two questions, explaining why the services are essential or not.

> **1** satellite dish **2** flip chart **3** computer **4** microphone
> **5** overhead projector **6** video conferencing equipment
> **7** slide projector **8** lectern

Professional practice: Faxes and emails

This exercise focuses on the language and style of faxes and emails, which can be written in the same way. Ask students about the advantages of these forms of correspondence compared to letters. (They arrive much more quickly and they're not likely to get lost on the way.) Tell students that they can be formal or informal depending on the relationship between writer and reader. In this case it is a formal fax. They need to be well organised and easy to read and the language and layout used are very specific. Students complete the phrases, using the fax on page 68 for reference. Elicit when to use *Yours sincerely* (after *Dear Mr / Mrs / Ms …*) or *Yours faithfully* (after *Dear Sir / Madam*). Refer students to the writing bank (students' book pages 111–112).

> * Sir, Miss
> * email / fax … interest in
>   pleasure … on … conference
> * have … questions … let me know
> * kind

Exercise 15, page 69

Look at exercise 15 as a class. In pairs / small groups, students make a floor plan (or use one of the plans in exercise 13) and decide which technical equipment and support services they want to offer (they can include all those mentioned before or choose the most essential). Students write their own faxes in groups or pairs, using the information given and the facilities they have chosen. They should organise their fax in the appropriate format, using the model on page 68 for reference. Pairs / groups can then write their faxes on suitable writing paper.

> **Extra Activity**
> Less advanced students can use one of the floor plans in exercise 13 and adapt the fax from Katarzyna Zarek as appropriate.

Workbook homework: exercises 7 and 8, page 43

P Photocopiable extra, page 87

This role-play involves clients looking for a venue for a business conference and two hotel representatives promoting their conference rooms as possible conference venues. The activity practises conference vocabulary and provides speaking practice.

Divide the class into groups of four, consisting of two hotel reps and two business managers. Give each student a role card from page 87. The reps read what conference facilities their hotels can offer and the managers read about their company and what facilities they require for their conferences.

Tell students that the reps have to promote their hotel as well as they can, with the aim being for the managers to choose their hotel as the conference venue rather than the other hotel. The managers choose the venue which they think will be more suitable, taking into account the facilities on offer and the way the rep dealt with them.

Within the groups of four, each manager speaks to each rep before deciding which venue they prefer. The managers tell the reps what kind of venue they are looking for and what facilities they need. The reps tell the managers what they can offer, including any optional extras.

At the end of the activity compare choices as a class. The managers explain the reasons why they chose one venue as opposed to the other.

Consolidation 2

Unit notes

The first two pages (exercises 1–6) revise and check the main grammar and vocabulary from units 6–10. The second spread (exercises 7–12) practises the skills from these units and students practise translating from English into their mother tongue. Exercises 1–3 can be set for homework, used as a test in class or done in pairs in class.

Exercise 1, page 70

Before looking at the exercise, elicit advice phrases and a sentence with each one to check that students know how to use them. Look at the advice phrases in exercise 1 and elicit a sentence with any phrases that were not elicited before. Students complete the exercise with the phrases. They should use each phrase once. Refer students to the language focus on page 48 and page 128 of the grammar reference.

> **1** a good idea to **2** best to **3** best not to **4** recommend
> **5** Avoid **6** shouldn't

Exercise 2, page 70

Elicit the different uses of the past simple and present perfect. Ask students a few comprehension questions so that they read the whole text first.

1 Where are Yukio and his friends travelling?
2 Where are they stopping on the way home?
3 Who does Yukio know in Paris?

Students then complete the exercise with the correct forms of the verbs in brackets. Refer students to the language focus on pages 26 (past simple) and 43 (present perfect) and to pages 126–127 of the grammar reference.

> **1** 've visited **2** did **3** stayed **4** haven't visited **5** won't
> be **6** have never been **7** went **8** has already been
> **9** drove **10** has worked **11** has lived

Exercise 3, page 71

Before students work in pairs, elicit the full questions. If some students have not been to a foreign country, they can talk about different places they have been to in their own country.

> The questions they should ask are:
> • How many foreign countries have you been to?
> • When did you go to ....?
> • How long did you stay there?
> • What did you do there?

Exercise 4, page 71

Students label the countries in pairs and think of one or two attractions for each country. Compare answers as a class. Ask students which of these countries they would most like to visit and why.

Exercise 5, page 71

Students plan their trips individually, recording the details on the form. They can do this for homework or in class. As they plan their itinerary, they should think carefully about the order in which they visit the countries and why they want to spend longer in one country than another, so that they can explain their reasons when they discuss their trips with other students.

Exercise 6, page 71

Students work in groups of six to talk about their plans. The purpose of this exercise is for students to find out where other students will be on certain days in order to see whether they will be able to meet up together. As this is a speaking exercise, make sure that students do not just read other students' itineraries, but ask each other questions, e.g. *Where will you be on Sunday 18 May? Will anyone be in Paris on Tuesday 20 May?*

Exercise 7, page 72

Students look at the different jobs and, in pairs, discuss what each person's job involves. They should then scan the advertisements and match them with the jobs, underlining where they find their answers. Ask students whether the advertisements make the jobs sound attractive. *Why?*

> **1** karaoke singer **2** tour guide and shark feeder
> **3** water sports instructor **4** trainee croupier
> **5** hospitality staff

Exercise 8, page 72

Students discuss the jobs in pairs to find out which one(s) they would most like to do and why. They can also discuss which one(s) they would least like to do. They can then discuss their preferences as a class to see which jobs are most / least popular.

Exercise 9, page 73

In this exercise, students adapt their CVs and write covering letters in application for the jobs advertised in exercise 7. It is best to set this exercise for homework; tell students to refer to the professional practice boxes and writing bank for help. Refer them to the professional practice boxes on pages 44 (CVs) and 45 (covering letters) and to pages 108 (CVs) and 109 (covering letters) of the writing bank.

Exercise 10, page 73

Before students translate the questions, ask them whether these questions are standard for interviews in their country. *Are the same structures used? If not, how are they different? Are the questions usually so formal or are they more direct?* Refer students to the professional practice box and read the tips as a class. Discuss why these points are important.

Students translate the questions in pairs, making sure that the translations sound natural and are not translated word for word. Compare translations as a class and discuss the differences between them. *Which translations are the most suitable and why? Are there any set phrases in their language which they can substitute for the English phrases?*

Professional practice: Translation

Make sure that students understand the meaning of *register*. (It is the words, style and language used by speakers and writers depending on the situation they find themselves; it may be formal, semi-formal, etc.) It is very important to use the appropriate register in both spoken and written language, otherwise you may sound offensive. The appropriate register for any given situation may vary from one language to another.

Also point out that the English language uses a lot of polite structures (e.g. modal verbs such as *can, could,* etc.), so when they make their translations they should decide whether the same politeness is appropriate in their language.

Exercise 11, page 73

In this exercise, students prepare interviews for the jobs applied for in exercise 9. Students exchange their CVs and applications with their partners. Give them plenty of time to prepare the interviews, following the instructions on page 73. This preparation can be done in class or at home. Refer them to exercise 17 on page 45 for help with the questions.

Extra Activity

If you think students will find it difficult to prepare the interviews individually, they can do it in small groups. Each group exchanges the job applications and CVs prepared in exercise 9 with a different group. They then prepare the interviews for the students in the other group following the instructions given in exercise 10, before dividing into pairs for exercise 11.

Exercise 12, page 73

Before students start the interviews, refer them to page 116, which gives tips for applicants, and give them time to read through the points. Students practise interviews in pairs before performing them in front of the class.

It is a good idea to record the interviews on cassette or video so that the recordings can be used to give feedback on language and appropriacy of manner.

The great outdoors

Fact File

Dorling Kindersley Eyewitness Travel Guide New Zealand

Websites:

http://travel.dk.com

www.travel-library.com/pacific/new_zealand (This site has a lot of information about adventure holidays in New Zealand, including interesting 'travelogues' in which people describe their trips there.)

www.nzholidays.co.nz (This site also has information about adventure holidays.)

Unit notes

Introduce the unit by asking students whether they know anything about New Zealand. Tell them that a lot of tourists go to New Zealand because of its greatly varied landscape and the large number of outdoor activities available. Ask them whether they can remember any of the adventure activities from unit 7. Ask them whether they can think of any more adventure sports related to mountains, rivers and the sky.

Exercise 1, page 74

Students look at the pictures of New Zealand and describe them in pairs. *Would you like to visit this country? What attracts you? What do you think you could do there?* In pairs, students talk about the various activities that they think people can do there on holiday. They then discuss what activities are associated with each geographical feature. These words can be difficult to pronounce, so help students with the pronunciation (see below).

Suggested answers:
- mountains: rock climbing, hiking, camping, abseiling, mountain biking
- rivers: canoeing, rafting, kayaking, fishing
- beaches: surfing, windsurfing, scuba diving, snorkelling, waterskiing, swimming
- lakes: fishing, sailing, power boating, windsurfing, waterskiing, jet skiing, swimming
- deserts: hiking, hot-air ballooning, 4x4 tours, camping, camel treks
- rainforests: wildlife spotting, hiking
- glaciers: skiing, snowboarding, snowmobiling

Pronunciation:
mountain /ˈmaʊntən‖ˈmaʊntn/
river /ˈrɪvə‖-ər/
lake /ləɪk/
beach /biːtʃ/
desert /ˈdezət‖-ərt/
rainforest /ˈreɪnˌfɒrəst/
glacier /ˈɡlæsiə‖ˈɡleɪʃər/

Ask students whether any of these geographical features occur anywhere in their country – and if so, where?

Exercise 2, page 74

Read the true / false statements. Can students answer any questions before reading the text? Students read the text on page 75 and answer the questions. Make sure that they underline the text where they find the answer and correct any false statements.

1 F (it is east of Australia) **2** F (the population is smaller) **3** T **4** F (Wellington is the capital) **5** T **6** T **7** T **8** F (there are thirteen)

Travel guide project

Putting your country on the map
Based on the map and description of New Zealand, students draw or find a map of their own country and write a description of its location and geographical features.

Exercise 3, page 75

Tell students that they are going to hear a conversation between a tourist information officer and a tourist in New Zealand. Before they listen, ask them whether there is anything that they would like to know about New Zealand. *What would you ask the information officer if you were the tourist?* Students listen and answer the questions.

See tapescript (students' book page 139).

1 Fox Glacier, Doubtful Sound, Mount Ruapebu
2 There are more sheep than people.
3 Tours to the fjords and glaciers.

Extra Activity

To simplify the listening exercise, give students a choice of answers. Listen and choose the correct answer.
1 Fox Glacier / Mount Tasman / Doubtful Sound Mount Ruapebu / Tongariro National Park
2 There are a lot more men than women. / There are more sheep than people. / More people live in the country than in the city.
3 Tours to: the fjords and glaciers / volcanoes / lakes and waterfalls

Exercise 4, page 75

Tell students that they are going to work in pairs. Student B works in the local tourist office, A is a tourist. Student B is going to sell a tour to student A and needs to do the job well if the tourist is to buy their tour. Refer students to the professional practice box before they start their preparation. The phrases will help group B to sell their tour.

Put students into A groups and B groups before they work in pairs so that they can prepare their information and questions together. Look on pages 119 and 123 for instructions. Group B students prepare the information together. If they are not sure of some facts or locations, they can invent them. Group A students prepare their questions. If necessary, they can refer to the tapescript between the tourist and the tourist officer on page 139 of the students' book to help them with the type of questions they could ask.

Students work in A / B pairs and practise their dialogues, including an appropriate beginning and ending, e.g.

B: Good morning. Can I help you?
A: Yes, please, I would like …

When they have completed the dialogues, ask group A whether they were given useful information and whether they were treated well by the tourist officer. *Would you buy the tour?*

Exercise 5, page 76

Tell students that they are going to hear someone making some changes to their tour booking. Look at the information on the booking form. This is the original booking that Mr Gould made with the travel company. Before listening to the CD / cassette, students predict what changes he may want to make, e.g. number of people, number of rooms, etc. This prediction will help students focus on the relevant information when listening to the dialogue. Students then listen and make the changes. Students can underline the changes the first time they listen and write the details during the second listening.

See tapescript (students' book pages 139–140).

pax: passengers

Number of pax: 13
Accommodation: 5 double rooms and 1 triple
Departure date: 24 March

Exercise 6, page 76

Students read the questions before listening again.

1 They're staying an extra day in Queenstown.
2 Flying to Auckland and then home to Scotland.
3 It is generally very punctual.

Extra Activity

Simplify the listening exercise by asking true / false questions:
1 They're staying an extra day in Christchurch. (F)
2 They're flying to Auckland before flying home. (T)
3 It is not always reliable. (F)

Language focus: Present tenses as future

Read the explanations and examples, highlighting the different uses according to whether we are referring to *timetables and schedules* or to *future plans and personal arrangements*.

See grammar reference section (students' book page 129).

Exercise 7, page 77

Students complete the sentences alone or in pairs. Tell them to take care with the third person singular in the present simple and with the question form in both tenses.

1 starts 2 're taking 3 does the Edinburgh train leave
4 're going on 5 does the hotel close 6 starts, doesn't finish 7 are you coming 8 is she doing

Exercise 8, page 77

Students look at Mr Gould's postcard and describe the picture briefly. Before they complete the text on the back of the postcard, set some comprehension questions so that students read through the whole text first. *When does their holiday finish? How long is their flight? Is their flight direct from New Zealand to Scotland? Who will be at the airport to meet them?*

Students complete the postcard with the appropriate tenses.

> **1** 're having **2** finishes **3** 're flying **4** doesn't leave **5** stops over **6** is meeting **7** 're staying **8** are you doing

Workbook homework: exercise 6, pages 46–47.

Extra Activity

Bring in some postcards, or pictures from magazines, of a variety of holiday locations. Students write postcards to each other from the places in their pictures. They should include the following information: *Where are they? How long are they staying? When are they leaving? What are their plans for the remaining days? Details of their flight home.*

Exercise 9, page 77

Students work in groups to find out about each other's plans. They should write their own plans before asking about each other's. They can invent information if they want to make it more interesting. Before they ask each other, elicit the question *What are you doing today?*. Students should reply in the present continuous and give complete answers. When they have information about the other students in their group, students report each other's plans to another group. In the new group, students decide whose plans and arrangements are the most interesting.

Extra Activity

Check that students know when a preposition is necessary and which one to use with each time expression.
- today / tomorrow
- *at* the weekend (UK) / *on* the weekend (US)
- this weekend
- *for* your next holiday
- *on* Tuesday
- *in* May
- *in* the afternoon

Exercise 10, page 78

Students look at the pictures and describe what is happening in each one. Ask them which of these activities they would like to do. *Have you done any of them? How would you feel in each situation? Can you be done in your country? Are they dangerous? Why do people do these kinds of activities?* Students then match the pictures with the types of excursions.

> **1** bungee jumping **2** mountain biking **3** whale watching **4** hot-air ballooning **5** rafting

Workbook homework: exercises 4 and 5, pages 45–46.

Exercise 11, page 78

Put students into A / B pairs to complete the information about the activities. Tell student A to turn to page 124. Students look at the information given and at the gaps. Elicit the questions that they need to ask each other in order to complete the missing information, e.g. *How long does … last? How much does … cost? What are the departure times for …? Which activity lasts for two hours and costs $125?*

Students check the information by comparing charts. Discuss the information briefly, e.g. *Which activity would you like to do? Is it expensive? Is enough time given for the activities?*

Exercise 12, page 78

Students work in groups of four using the information on the page. Each group decides which activities they think are most enjoyable for a group of young people and what combination of activities would make an exciting and varied itinerary. They then plan their itineraries and present them to the rest of their class.

Workbook homework: exercises 1 and 2, pages 44–45.

Professional practice: Confirming and checking

Read the information in the professional practice box as a class, emphasising the four points. Ask students why each point is important. *Why is it so important to check certain information?* (Suggested answer: it is easy to make mistakes with numbers and spelling, especially over the phone.)

Exercise 13, page 79

Briefly review the letters of the alphabet, especially the letters that are easily confused by your students. Tell students that they are going to hear five short dialogues in which numbers and names are being checked.

Students listen and complete the missing information. Repeat as necessary. Students compare answers before checking as a class. Check students' spelling as they read out their answers.

See tapescript (students' book page 140).

> 1 BGI 0277 2 Doherty 3 3095 5541 8409 1057
> 4 BED 099415-02 5 paradise@travelnet.com

Exercise 14, page 79

Students match the questions and answers individually and check with the CD / cassette. They then take it in turns to ask and answer the questions. Encourage students to give the answers at a reasonable speed: not too fast for the listener to write down and not so slow as to sound inefficient.

> 1 c 2 a 3 e 4 b 5 d

Extra Activity

Put students into A / B pairs. Either students dictate their own information to their partner, or student A sits with his / her back to the board, student B facing the board. Student A needs a pen and paper. Write a combination of numbers and letters on the board (see below). Student B dictates what you have written and student A writes it down. Check answers. Change over so that A can now see the board and dictates to student B. If your students like a bit of competition, make it into a race and see which pair finishes first. NB The answers must be correct, so both speed and accuracy are necessary.

Student B dictates:
656 879 302
G-A-M-L-E-Y
julia.jones@retemail.es
XV80560311
31st January 1965

Student A dictates:
722 950 0495
P-I-E-R-C-E
george.smythe@msc.gr
YJ7990521
12th May 1975

Exercise 15, page 79

Tell students that they are going to prepare a dialogue between a travel agent and a customer who wants to change his / her booking. It is a good idea to refer back to the tapescript on pages 139–140 of the students' book to remind students of useful expressions that they can use in

their dialogues. Student A (travel agent) turns to page 119 and student B (customer) turns to page 123.

Give students time to read their instructions and to plan what they want to say before they start. Elicit some expressions that they can use in their dialogues, e.g.

Travel agent:
How can I help you?
Do you have your confirmation form with you, sir / madam?
Just let me check.
I'll just confirm those changes.
I'll send you a fax to confirm those changes.
That's now confirmed.
I'll make that change for you.

Customer:
I need to make some changes to my booking.
We'd prefer to …
And another thing …

Make sure that student A knows that he / she needs to make the necessary changes to the booking form.

Extra Activity

The travel agents can prepare their questions together while the customers prepare what they want to say before you set up the A / B pairs.

Exercise 16, page 79

Students practise writing a fax / email to confirm the changes made to the booking in exercise 15. Student A and student B write the fax together in class or individually for homework. To help them write their faxes / emails, refer students to pages 111 and 112 of the writing bank. If you set this for homework, ask students to send it to the school's email address if possible.

Workbook homework: exercise 7, page 47.

Extra Activity

Ask students whether they would recommend New Zealand as a holiday destination. *Who would you recommend to go there and which places / activities would you recommend?*

Winter holidays

what clues helped them choose their answers. They then comment on which of these jobs they would like to do.

See tapescript (coursebook page 140).

UNIT OBJECTIVES

Professional practice: selling optional extras, giving directions, replying to emails
Language focus: giving instructions, the passive
Vocabulary: ski equipment, entertainment

Fact File

http://travel.dk.com
www.skinet.com

Unit notes

Introduce the theme of winter holidays by asking students whether they have ever been skiing. *If so, did you enjoy it? Would you recommend it? What advice would you give to first-time skiers? If not, would you like to try it? Why / why not? Do you think it would be easy?*

Exercise 1, page 80

Ask students to look at the picture in pairs and to describe what the people are doing. If necessary, explain the difference between *downhill* and *cross-country skiing*. Brainstorm other winter sports such as *skating, snowmobiling, tobogganing, curling, ice hockey, snowboarding,* etc., and ask students which of these activities they would prefer to do.

Exercise 2, page 80

Students match the pictures with the words and describe each item. Ask them what the purpose of each item is.

1 chairlift **2** helmet **3** goggles **4** gloves **5** bindings **6** skis **7** ski pass **8** snowboard **9** cable car **10** poles **11** boots **12** ski jacket **13** drag lift

Workbook homework: exercise 4, page 49.

Exercise 3, page 80

Before playing the CD / cassette, look at the ski resort jobs in the vocabulary box. Ask students what they think each job involves. Tell them that they are going to hear five short conversations at a ski resort. They have to listen and decide who is speaking in each extract. Students listen and match the speakers with the jobs. Ask them

1 ski hire shop assistant **2** chairlift attendant **3** ski instructor **4** resort representative (rep) **5** cafeteria staff

Exercise 4, page 80

Students read the questions carefully before listening again. In pairs, they try to answer some of the questions either by predicting the answers or by remembering any information from the previous listening. They then listen again and answer the questions.

1 boots, skis, poles, bindings **2** lower the safety bar **3** turn left **4** in the hotel lounge **5** sandwiches and drinks

Workbook homework: exercises 1 and 2, pages 48–49.

Language focus: Giving instructions

Before referring to the language focus, ask students to look at the tapescript on page 140 of the students' book. Tell them that speakers 1, 2 and 3 are all giving instructions to skiers. Elicit speaker 1's instruction, i.e. *Go over there*. Then elicit the instructions that the other two speakers give. Ask students to underline these instructions.

Write down examples on the board and elicit which verb form is used when giving instructions (the imperative). Refer students to the language focus to check their answer.

See grammar reference section (students' book page 130).

Workbook homework: exercise 7, page 51.

Exercise 5, page 81

Tell students that the imperative is also used for giving directions. Students look at the directions in the box and match them to the pictures showing different directions.

1 go straight on **2** go downstairs **3** go right **4** go upstairs **5** go left

Exercise 6, page 81

Look at the floor plan of the ski lodge at the bottom of the page and check that students know the names of the different places shown. Tell students that they are going to practise asking for and giving directions. Elicit how they can ask for directions politely:

Excuse me, could you tell me the way to …?

Could you tell me how to get to…?

Where is the …, please?

Put students into A / B pairs. Check *left* and *right* before they start; many people confuse the two. Student A turns to page 120 and asks for directions to each place. They then change roles. Check directions as a class.

> *lounge*: a comfortable public room in a hotel with armchairs and sofas. There is often a TV there.
> *locker room*: a room in a hotel, sports building, school, etc. where people change their clothes and leave them in small lockable cupboards (*lockers*)
> *rep*: abbreviation for *representative*

Exercise 7, page 82

Ask students about sport in their country in general: *Which sports are the most popular? Is there a national sport? Are you interested in sport?*

Elicit special sporting events around the world, e.g. the Olympic Games, Football World Cup, Wimbledon Championships, etc. *Have any events like these taken place in your country?* If so, students discuss in pairs what preparations are / were made. If not, they discuss in pairs what preparations need to be made for such events.

> Suggested answers:
> • Build new stadia and accommodation
> • Organise extra accommodation
> • Increase security, e.g. more police
> • Close some areas of the city
> • Provide more public transport
> • Offer more language learning facilities, especially English, so that the host country / city can deal with people from all over the world

Exercise 8, page 82

Tell students that they are going to read an article about the 2002 Winter Olympics in Salt Lake City. First ask students whether they watched the event on TV. Before they read the webpage, point out that it was written *before* the Salt Lake games started.

Read the three titles and elicit what information they would expect to read in an article with these titles. Tell students to skim-read the text. They only need to know the general contents to find the most suitable title. Students should give reasons for their choice of title. If they do not agree with each other, discuss as a class which title is most suitable and why.

NB The article comes from a US website so some of the vocabulary is US English. Tell students that they need to be aware that although the same language is spoken in these countries, there are some differences between US and UK English. See the vocabulary box on page 82 of the coursebook.

> No hotel rooms for Winter Games ('it's a little too late to look for hotel rooms…', 'most of the city's hotel rooms were booked some time ago…', etc.).

> *condominium* (US): a building containing several apartments / one of the apartments in this building. Usually abbreviated to *condo*.
> *sponsor*: a person or company that helps finance the organisation of an event in exchange for the right to advertise at the event
> *lodging*: a place to stay

Exercise 9, page 82

Students read the text again to answer the true / false questions, underlining where they find their answers in the text. *Are you surprised by any of the information in the article?*

> **1** F (it is very difficult) **2** T **3** T **4** F (12,000 / 60% of 20,000) **5** F ($150 to more than $3,000 per night) **6** T

Workbook homework: exercise 3, page 49.

Language focus: The passive

Choose one passive sentence from the text and write it on the board. Ask students which structure is used. *How is it constructed? When is it used?* Check the language focus box for answers and refer to the grammar reference section on page 130 of the coursebook.

Workbook homework: exercises 5 and 6, page 50.

Exercise 10, page 83

Before completing the text with the passive, ask comprehension questions so that students read through the whole text first:

1 What is SHMS? (Swiss Hotel Management School)

2 Where is it? (Montreux)

3 How many languages are spoken in Switzerland? (Three)

4 Is hotel management training new to Switzerland? (No, it has 'a long and reputable history for management training').

Ask them whether they would like to go to this school. *Why / why not?*

Elicit construction of the passive in the present and past. Write on the board.

Present: *is / are* + past participle

Past: *was / were* + past participle

Students complete the text individually or in pairs.

> **1** is located **2** is divided **3** is spoken **4** is spoken
> **5** are accommodated **6** were / are trained **7** are
> recognised **8** are placed

Exercise 11, page 83

Write the two phonetic symbols on the board. Ask whether students know which sounds they represent. If they do, elicit a word with each sound; if not, write *the* below / ð / and *think* below / θ /. Play the CD / cassette. Students listen and repeat to make sure they can hear and produce both sounds. They then listen and decide which sound is in each of the words in the box. Check and then listen and repeat each sound.

> /ð/ this, weather, clothes, there
> /θ/ thanks, thing, thirty, fifth

Extra Activity
Explain to students that both sounds are produced with the same mouth shape but /ð/ is voiced, whereas /θ/ is not. Students should be able to feel the vibration in their throats with the voiced /ð/ sound.
Write this sentence on the board:
This is the thirty-fifth weather change this month.
Students underline all the *th* sounds and practise saying the sentence. To make it more fun, see who can say it the fastest without making any mistakes.

Workbook homework: exercise 8, page 51.

Exercise 12, page 83

Students work in groups of four to plan their Olympic Games. They should make their plans and give reasons for their choices of location, transport, etc. Dicuss ideas as a class and decide together which ideas are the most suitable.

Extra Activity
When a country decides to bid to host the Olympic Games, various cities usually compete to become the country's official bid. Put students into groups and give each group a city in their country. Each group then has to draw up a plan for hosting the Olympic Games in that city, then present it to the class. Students should review the professional practice advice on page 56 of the students' book to help them with their presentations. The best presentation is adopted as the country's official bid for the next Olympics. Depending on the country, students choose to bid for either the summer or winter Olympics.

Exercise 13, page 84

In pairs, students discuss the possible entertainment and activities on a skiing holiday. Think about day- and night-time activities for different age groups (children, teenagers, adults). Students share their ideas with the rest of the class and decide which ideas would be most popular for holidaymakers.

> Suggested answers: excursions, cross-country skiing, torch-lit processions, night skiing, sledging, snowmobiles, ski lessons, competitions, quizzes, discos, parties, karaoke, children's games, etc.

Exercise 14, page 84

Students look at the entertainment vocabulary first before reading the definitions. Let them give their own definitions for words that they already know. It is good for students to practise using their own words to explain what something means before they see a dictionary definition. Then ask them to match the words with the definitions and check their answers.

> **1** b **2** g **3** a **4** e **5** f **6** h **7** d **8** c

Pronunciation
exhibition /ˌeksɪˈbɪʃən/ the *h* is silent
quiz /kwɪz/
live /laɪv/ *band* 'live' is an adjective here and is pronounced differently from the verb *to live* /lɪv/

To help students remember the words, prepare
Pelmanism cards for the next lesson: write the
entertainment words on individual cards of one
colour, and the definitions on individual cards of
another colour. Prepare enough sets of cards for
students to play in small groups.
Put the cards face down so that the writing cannot be
seen. Student A (or pair A) picks up a word card first,
gives the definition, and then picks up a definition
card. If the definition matches the word, student A
keeps the pair of cards. If they do not match, he / she
puts the cards back in the same place face down. Now
it is student B's turn. Student B does the same: picks
up a word card first, gives the definition and then
picks up a definition card. And so on. Students need
to remember which cards are where so that they can
find the pairs. The student (or pair) with the most
pairs of cards at the end is the winner.
Teach students useful games expressions like:
It's my / your turn / go.
Whose turn is it?
Don't cheat!

Exercise 15, page 84

Tell students that they are going to hear a resort rep
describing an entertainment programme to
holidaymakers. Look at the programme before listening.
Students listen and complete the missing events. Check
answers and ask what they think of the programme. *Is it
interesting / varied? Does it offer enough activities for
different age groups? What would you like to do if you were
there?*

See tapescript (students' book page 141).

Extra Activity
To simplify the first listening, tell students what the
events are (see answers below). Students then listen
and put the events in order.
Ask more advanced students to say what they think
Melanie's lifestyle would be like as a ski rep. *Would
you like to do it?*

1 Welcome meeting **2** Cross-country skiing
3 Snowshoeing **4** Demonstration of ski equipment
5 Torchlit descent of the mountain **6** Party / Karaoke

Exercise 16, page 84

Students read the questions carefully before listening
again. Let them listen twice before comparing their
answers with a partner. Check as a class.

1 in the hotel lounge **2** must be over twelve and
accompanied by an adult **3** snow trekking, wearing
'tennis rackets' on your feet **4** in the hotel lobby
5 advanced skiers **6** live band, dancing and karaoke
7 on the noticeboard in the hotel lobby

Extra Activity
To simplify the listening task, make the questions into
true / false statements.
1 *The welcome meeting is in the bar.* (F)
2 *Children must be over sixteen to go
cross-country skiing.* (F)
3 *'Snowshoeing' is trekking in snow with special
shoes that look like tennis rackets.* (T)
4 *The demonstration of new ski equipment is
in the hotel lobby.* (T)
5 *Everybody can take part in the torchlit descent
of the mountain.* (F)
6 *There will be a live band and dancing for the
farewell party.* (T)
7 *People should sign up for the activities on the
noticeboard in the hotel lounge.* (F)

Professional practice: Selling optional extras

The phrases presented here are useful tips for holiday reps
to promote extra activities.

Fact File

Some holidaymakers may just want to ski all day and
then relax and sleep at night. Others, however, want to
do a lot of different things as well as skiing. For some,
the extra activities and social events are as important
or even more important than the skiing itself and are
known as *après-ski*. Therefore ski resorts always offer
a variety of optional extra activities. These activities
may be advertised in the holiday brochure or on
arrival at the resort and need to be promoted so that
people sign up for them.
These extras are an important source of income for
the tour operator, the local travel agent and the ski
resort employees, and a lot of time and effort are
usually put into the organising and advertising of
them.

Read the professional practice tips and discuss the information. *Why are these phrases and tips useful?* (If you are enthusiatic and show interest in customers, they are more likely to be enthusiastic and interested too.)

Exercise 17, page 85

Now it is the students' turn to prepare a programme of events for holidaymakers at their resort and to promote it. Read the instructions in the students' book and highlight the point that they are in competition with Melanie and the other reps in the class. Therefore they need to prepare an interesting and varied programme and to present it in the best way to attract custom. Give groups plenty of time to prepare their programme and to decide how they wish to present it. They can use some of the same activities that Melanie offers, together with their own ideas. They should refer to the professional practice box when planning their presentations and to the tapescript on page 141 if necessary.

Each group gives their presentation. Everyone can vote for the best programme and presentation, giving reasons for their choice. It is always useful for students to give each other feedback in order to improve their work.

Extra Activity
Arrange the classroom so that the presentations are given in what resembles a hotel lobby / lounge, i.e. with the reps at the front and the holidaymakers sitting around. Allow the holidaymakers to ask questions about the different activities and to react to the information given, e.g. laugh, cheer, make appropriate sounds, as in exercise 15 on the CD / cassette.

Exercise 18, page 85

Tell students that they are going to write an email in reply to a tour operator who may be interested in the entertainment programme that they prepared in exercise 17. Read the email from Julie Linden and ask what information they need to include in the reply (details of programme, times and prices). Students prepare their replies in groups. Refer them to the model email in the writing bank on page 112 of the students' book for help with layout and expressions.

Extra Activity
Ask students what they think it would be like to be a rep for winter holidays or to be involved in the preparation and organisation of an Olympic Winter Games.

P Photocopiable extra, see page 88

In this exercise, students practise selling optional extras and persuading tourists on a week's skiing holiday to do some optional activities.

Divide the class into groups of eight, with four tourists and four reps from rival agencies in each group. The reps, who are in competition with each other, each have a number of activities / excursions to promote and sell for which they will get ten percent commission if they are successful. Meanwhile, the tourists have a limited amount of money which they have to spend: $250. The reps take it in turns to talk to each tourist individually and tell them about what they have to offer. Remind the reps of the tips in the professional practice box on page 85 of the students' book. The tourists make a note of the activities / excursions they are interested in and once they have spoken to all the reps, make their final choices.

When each tourist in the group has decided what they are going to choose, check as a group to see how much commission each rep has made. The rep who makes the most commission is the winner.

Spend a few minutes' feedback time at the end of the exercise for the different groups to compare results and for the tourists to explain why they chose some extras and not others. Was it because of the activity itself, the price, or that the rep was not persuasive enough?

If there is time, repeat the exercise with the students changing roles and groups.

⑬ Land of smiles

<table>
<tr><td colspan="2">UNIT OBJECTIVES</td></tr>
<tr><td>Professional practice:</td><td>giving health and safety advice</td></tr>
<tr><td>Language focus:</td><td>relative pronouns</td></tr>
<tr><td>Vocabulary:</td><td>ecotourism, medical kit, word-building, US / UK English</td></tr>
</table>

Fact File

Dorling Kindersley Eyewitness Travel Guide Thailand
Websites: http://travel.dk.com
http://www.asiatravel.com/thaiinfo.html (This website has a lot of information about all aspects of tourism in Thailand.)

Unit notes

Introduce the unit by asking students what they know about Thailand and what attracts people there on holiday. *Do you know anyone who has been there? Would they like to go there? Why is the title of the unit 'Land of smiles'? What does it suggest about Thailand?*

Fact File

Thailand has been a popular holiday destination for many years. Holidaymakers are attracted by the beaches, landscape, opportunities to go trekking and the warm welcome with which they are greeted by the Thai people. Thai people are famous for their friendliness, hence the title of the unit. The most popular tourist destinations are Bangkok (the capital), Chiang Mai in the north and Phuket in the south.

Exercise 1, page 86

Students look at the pictures of the activities and describe them in pairs. *Which activities appeal to you? Which ones would you not like to do?* In pairs students discuss the benefits and problems that tourism can bring to a country. Compare ideas as a class and write them on the board. Discuss which ideas are most beneficial and which ones are most problematic for a country.

Suggested answers
1 sightseeing **2** local customs and festivals **3** elephant riding
- Benefits: money, jobs, economic growth and opportunity for the country to develop
- Problems: pollution, exploitation and destruction of local environment, culture and way of life

Exercise 2, page 86

Before students match the vocabulary and definitions, ask them what they understand by the term *ecotourism. In what ways do you think tourism can be eco-friendly? Is it a popular type of tourism in your country?* Students look at the words and match them with their definitions, using a dictionary where necessary.

1 b 2 f 3 d 4 c 5 a 6 g 7 h 8 e

As some of the words are long, ask students to mark the main stress on each word and to practise saying them.

Exercise 3, page 86

Tell students that they are going to read a text about ecotourism in Thailand. Before reading, students should look at the possible answers a–c. Emphasise that they should read the text quickly to find the answer. They do not need to read every word carefully. Students should than compare answers and give reasons for their choice.

Answer: a

Exercise 4, page 86

This time they need to read the text carefully in order to answer the comprehension questions. After checking the answers as a class, students give their opinion on ecotourism as described in the text.

> 1 It damages the ecosystem and the living and working conditions of local people.
> 2 Tourists throw rubbish into the sea.
> 3 They have limited the number of mountain trekkers to only thirty per month.
> 4 It includes food, accommodation, sightseeing and a donation to the community.
> 5 So that they can attract more tourists.
> 6 The tourists.

Workbook homework: exercises 1–3, pages 52–53.

Exercise 5, page 87

Look at the verb / noun table as a class and read the example of the verb *damage* and the noun *damage*. Tell students that when they learn a new word, it is useful to learn other words with the same root too. The words missing from the table are in the text in the same order. Students scan the text for the missing words and complete the table.

> 1 damage 2 solution 3 benefit 4 conservation
> 5 protect 6 donation 7 attract 8 destroy

Exercise 6, page 87

Ask students whether they think that tourists / people in general usually respect public signs. Students discuss the questions in groups of four and then compare their answers as a class.

Exercise 7, page 88

Tell students that they are going to read some statements about Thai culture and discuss whether they are true or false. Tell them not to worry if they do not know the answers. The purpose of this exercise is for them to discuss the statements together and guess the answers. It will then be easier for them to answer the questions when they read the text.

Students then read the text and answer the questions, underlining where they find the answers in the text and correcting the false statements. After checking the answers, ask students whether they are surprised by any of the information. *Is the information interesting / useful for tourists? Would you feel comfortable visiting Thailand? What else would you like to know about this country?* If they would like to know more about Thailand, they can visit the websites mentioned in the introduction to this unit (page 61).

> 1 T 2 F (they are very tolerant and avoid arguments)
> 3 T 4 F (copy the person who is greeting you) 5 F (never touch someone's head) 6 T 7 F (most teenage boys become monks) 8 F (take off your shoes)

> *get on with*: have a good relationship with
> *taboos*: religious or social customs which forbid a particular activity because it is offensive

Language focus: Defining relative pronouns

Defining relative clauses are used to define / identify people or things. The relative pronouns *which, who* and *that* are used to introduce defining relative clauses. No commas are necessary.

Students complete the information with the help of the examples.

> • *which, that* or *who*
> • *which* or *that* for objects and *who* or *that* for people

Refer students to the grammar reference (students' book page 130).

Exercise 8, page 89

Students work in pairs to match the sentence halves.

> 1 b 2 c 3 e 4 d 5 a

Language focus: Non-defining relative pronouns

Relative clauses can also be used to give extra information about people or things. They are called non-defining relative clauses and are introduced by the non-defining relative pronouns *which* and *who*. Commas are used in non-defining relative clauses.

Students look at the examples to see where the commas are needed. They underline all the relative pronouns in the text on page 88 and say whether they are defining or non-defining.

Examples in text:
- *The Thais, <u>who</u> are very friendly and helpful, …* (non-defining)
- *The Thai greeting, <u>which</u> is known as the* Wai, … (non-defining)
- *an ancient greeting <u>that</u> used to show…* (defining)
- *… just copy the person <u>who</u> is greeting you* (defining)
- *Never touch someone's head, <u>which</u> is the most sacred part of the body for Thais, …* (non-defining) *etc.*

Refer students to the grammar reference (students' book page 130).

Workbook homework: exercises 5 and 6, page 54.

Exercise 9, page 89

Ask students to look at the sentences in pairs and to decide whether the information given is defining the person / thing or giving us extra information about it. They then underline the relative pronouns and decide where to put the commas when necessary.

1 The *Wai*, <u>which</u> is the traditional greeting, involves putting your palms together. (non-defining)
2 It is illegal to criticise the Royal family, <u>which</u> is the most important institution in Thailand. (non-defining)
3 Foreigners <u>who</u> are used to quick service shouldn't show impatience or they will be ignored by waiters. (defining) *With commas the sentence would become a non-defining clause which would mean that **all** foreigners are used to quick service.*
4 Monks, <u>who</u> never return the *Wai* greeting, are very respected in Thailand. (non-defining)
5 … Thais believe that one of nine spirits <u>that</u> inhabit a building lives in the threshold. (defining)
6 The Thai national anthem, <u>which</u> is played twice a day in public parks and buildings, is also played before cinema performances. (non-defining)

Exercise 10, page 89

Students can do this exercise in pairs or small groups. Ask some additional questions for them to discuss:
Are etiquette and customs the same for different age groups / parts of the country?
Have they changed since their grandparents were young? Are they still strong or are some being lost?
Which ones are the most important for foreigners to know so that they do not offend local people?
Are there any customs that have come from abroad, e.g. via TV from the US?

Travel guide project

Etiquette and customs
If etiquette and customs are an important part of their culture, students can write a description about them to add to their projects. They can use the information discussed in exercise 10 and any information they can find in books or on the internet to write their descriptions. If they need help organising their descriptions, they can follow the categories in the students' book. They can also include sections in answer to the additional questions. They should write a brief introduction and conclusion to the descriptions.

Exercise 11, page 90

Tell students that they are going to listen to someone booking a holiday in Thailand. Read the questions and before playing the CD / cassette for the first time, refer students to the professional tips. When they listen to the dialogue they should bear the tips in mind in order to help them decide whether or not the travel agent is good at selling. Remind students that they do not need to understand everything that is being said at first.

See tapescript (students' book page 141).

- Insurance.
- Yes, he is good because he explains the benefits of the insurance, he is well-informed, answers questions, is polite and persuades the customer to take the insurance.

Exercise 12, page 90

Ask students why it is important to take out travel insurance when you go on holiday. *When might you need it? What does it normally cover? Have you ever needed it when you have been on holiday?* Read the questions before listening again. Students listen and answer the questions.

1 Full health and travel insurance.
2 It meets the customer's specific needs.
3 High-risk activities, full costs for medical treatment, accidents and helicopter evacuation.
4 Immediately.
5 Cancelled flights, stolen or lost cash, credit cards, passport or luggage.
6 £17.50

Workbook homework: exercise 9, page 55.

Exercise 13, page 90

Look at the pictures of the contents of the medical / first-aid kit. Students name what they can before looking at the vocabulary box. In pairs, they discuss what they normally take with them on holiday and whether they usually need these things. Students label the items in pairs, discuss their uses and say whether they are necessary for all types of holidays.

1   plasters (if you have a small cut)
2   aspirin (if you have a cold or headache)
3   mosquito repellent (to stop mosquitoes biting you)
4   tweezers (to extract something under your skin)
5   thermometer (to check your temperature)
6   pocketknife (to cut something)
7   sunblock (to protect your skin from the sun)
8   scissors (to cut a bandage or plaster)
9   bandage (if you have a large cut or a sprain)
10 antiseptic cream (to prevent infection)

Workbook homework: exercise 7, page 54.

Exercise 14, page 90

Ask students to read the advertisement for the trekking trip in Thailand. They should discuss what kind of preparations they would have to make before doing a trip like this. *What kind of people would do it? What would it be like to do a trip like this? Would you like to do it? Why / why not?*

Students make their lists of clothes and equipment to take on a trek individually before discussing them in small groups. Point out that they would have to carry their packs for three days so they should consider the weight of the things on their packing list. *Do you agree with each other about what you would take? Is anyone in your group taking anything that you consider unnecessary?*

Extra Activity

Further speaking practice: prioritising items.
Each student chooses ten items of clothing and equipment to take trekking. They should choose the items that they think are the most important. Next they work in pairs and choose ten items together. If they do not agree with each other, they must convince each other why some things are more important than others. They can have no more than ten items between them. They then join another pair, and must now choose items between the four. Continue in this way until the whole class is working together to reach consensus. Finally as a class they must decide on the ten most important things. Change the number of items if you prefer.

Extra Activity

Revise the vocabulary in the next class with the memory game 'In my medical kit I packed a ...'. Play it either in groups or as a class. Student 1 begins with 'In my medical kit I packed a penknife' (for example). Student 2 continues 'In my medical kit I packed a penknife and some aspirin' (for example). Student 3 continues in the same way, repeating the full list of all the previous items and adding another item from the medical kit. And so on around the group / class. Continue as long as they can. If you want to make the game competitive, add this rule: if a student makes a mistake, cannot remember an item or mispronounces a word, he / she is out. Continue until the last person is out.

Exercise 15, page 90

Tell students that it is a good idea to get expert advice before doing a trip like this so that you know what to take with you. Tell them that they are going to hear someone advising tourists what to pack. Students read the instructions to the exercise, then listen and tick the items they hear on their list. Check as a class and ask whether they had the appropriate clothes and equipment on their packing lists. *What necessary items did they omit? What unnecessary items did they include?*

Students compare their answers in groups to see who was the most practical and best prepared for the trip and who was the least practical.

See tapescript (students' book pages 141–142).

- small rucksack
- trainers / lightweight trekking boots
- two cotton T-shirts
- two pairs of shorts
- two pairs of socks
- small towel / sarong
- swimsuit
- toiletries
- simple medical kit
- sun cream
- hat
- sunglasses
- sweater and long trousers / tracksuit
- small torch
- camera and film
- mosquito repellent
- long-sleeved shirt

To simplify the listening exercise, give students a long list of items. Students then listen and tick the ones they hear, making any changes necessary, e.g. to the quantity of an item.

The items below are in order on the CD / cassette with some extra items added and a few changes to the quantities. Tell them that there are eight differences. The corrections are in italics below.

big rucksack (*small rucksack*)
sleeping bag ✗
trainers / lightweight trekking boots ✔
four cotton T-shirts *(two)*
two pairs of shorts ✔
three pairs of socks *(two)*
big towel / sarong *(small)*
swimsuit ✔
toiletries ✔
simple medical kit ✔
sun cream ✔
hat ✔
waterproof jacket ✗
sunglasses ✔
sweater ✔
long trousers / tracksuit ✔
tent ✗
small torch ✔
camera and film ✔
binoculars ✗
mosquito repellent ✔
long-sleeved shirt ✔

Workbook homework: exercise 4, page 53.

Exercise 16, page 91

Before listening again, students read the questions carefully and predict possible answers. They then listen and answer.

1 waterfall, villages **2** hot during the day, chilly at night, no rain **3** small risk of malaria

After checking answers, students discuss the trek in pairs. *Does it sound interesting / exciting? Would you like to do it? What do you know about malaria? Would you worry about getting it?*

When travelling to countries like Thailand, tourists are recommended to have vaccinations against certain diseases, e.g. typhoid and cholera, and to take malaria tablets before, during and some time after their trip. They are also advised not to drink water unless it is from a sealed bottle and to be careful with fresh fruit and vegetables as they may have been washed in infected water.

Exercise 17, page 91

Remind students of the differences between US and UK English. Ask whether they can remember any differences from previous units, e.g. *check* (US) and *bill* (UK).

Students may use dictionaries to help match the words.

1 b **2** d **3** a **4** e **5** c

The word *torch* also exists in US English but it has a different meaning.
UK English: a hand-held electric light that runs on batteries
US English: a long stick with a burning flame at the end
So do not ask for a *torch* if you are in a national park or wooded area in the US; ask for a *flashlight* or they will think that you want to set fire to the park!

Professional practice: Giving health advice

Read the phrases as a class and highlight when to use the bare infinitive / *to* + infinitive, gerund or imperative / *in case* + present simple. They will need to use these expressions in exercises 18 and 19.

Exercise 18, page 91

Give students enough time to read the safety advice and to think of how they can give advice to their partners. They should also think about how they can ask for advice. Students work in pairs asking for and giving appropriate advice. They should use a variety of the expressions in the professional practice box.

Workbook homework: exercise 8, page 55.

Exercise 19, page 91

This exercise can be done in pairs. Students should use the following structure to prepare their leaflets:

1 general introduction similar to the descriptions in the students' book
2 divide the advice into the categories in exercise 18, e.g. personal safety, etc.
3 brief conclusion / general tip

Travel guide project

Travelling in your country
Students can add the leaflets prepared in exercise 19 to their projects.

Extra Activity
Ask students to summarise what Thailand has to offer, what recommendations they would give to people planning to go there and whether it is a good holiday destination.

P. Photocopiable extra, see page 89

These photocopiable cards double up as a Pelmanism matching game and a whole class mingling speaking activity. You may choose to do one or both, in either order.

Pelmanism matching game:

Divide the class into groups of four or six and then into pairs within each group. Give each group a cut-up copy of the injuries and the items from the medical kit. Each group divides the cards into the two categories and places them face down on the table without looking at what is written on each card. Tell them to place the injuries on one side of the table and the medical kit items on the other.

One person from each pair takes it in turns to pick up first an injury card and then a medical kit card. Before picking up the medical card, they must say what the corresponding medical kit item is. If they do not know, they cannot pick up the second card. If they find the corresponding card, they keep the card; if not they put both cards back where they took them from, again face down.

Students must concentrate and try to remember where the cards are placed.

The winning pair is the pair that has collected the most cards.

Mingling activity:

Give each student either an injury card or a medical kit card which they must not show to anyone. The students with the injury cards go around the class telling people what their problem is and asking other students whether they can help them. When they find someone who has the necessary items to help them, they sit down together and the 'medic' gives advice to the 'patient', using expressions like *It's best to …, You shouldn't …, Make sure you …,* etc.

Enjoy your stay

Fact File

Dorling Kindersley Eyewitness Travel Guide
  St Petersburg
http://travel.dk.com
http://col-ed.org/echo2001/echo2001_russialinks.html

Unit notes

Ask students what they know about Russia. Students look at the pictures of people staying at hotels and describe them in pairs. What do they think this unit is going to focus on?

Fact File

St Petersburg, which is Russia's second largest city after Moscow, is situated in the northwest corner of the country. Like Amsterdam and Venice, it is a 'water city' as it spreads over more than forty islands separated by a network of rivers and canals. Rich in history and considered one of the most beautiful cities in Europe, St Petersburg attracts tourists interested in visiting the baroque monasteries and neo-classical palaces and enjoying the stunning scenery. The top attractions of the city are the Russian Museum, the Hermitage and the Church of Spilled Blood.

Exercise 1, page 92

Before starting this exercise it is a good idea to check the exchange rate of the rouble against the local currency (e.g. at http://finance.yahoo.com/m3) so that you have an idea of the prices on the bill. (At the time of writing there were 32 Russian roubles to the US dollar.) Then students can decide whether or not the items on the bill are expensive compared to their country.

Elicit *bill* and *check* (US). Ask what expenses students expect to find on a hotel bill apart from the room itself. Look at the bill and compare with students' own answers. Ask whether it is an expensive hotel. *Do the extras cost a lot? What other extras are usually added?*

Suggested answers:
local tax or VAT (value added tax); service charge; restaurant; minibar; telephone; pay TV; room service; business service; laundry

Exercise 2, page 92

Before playing the CD / cassette, check that students remember the meaning of *checking out* and what happens when guests check out of a hotel. Read the instructions in the students' book. Give clues to Mr Collins' reaction: ask whether he might be happy / angry / surprised. *Why might he feel this way?* Students listen and answer the questions.

He reacts badly because he is surprised by the additional charges: the local tax (7%) and the 5% surcharge when paying by credit card. He has also forgotten the telephone call he made to the UK.

Exercise 3, page 92

Before playing the CD / cassette again, read the questions carefully and ask students to predict some of the answers, e.g. *What did he order from room service? Who might he call while he is away on business?*

1 a chicken sandwich and a pot of coffee
2 in the hotel information pack in each room
3 his wife in the UK
4 because they are made via satellite
5 10,783 roubles
6 by cash

Workbook homework: exercises 1, 2 and 3, pages 56–57.

Exercise 4, page 93

Elicit what the type of money a particular country uses is called: *currency. What is the currency in your country? How is it abbreviated?*

Tell students to work in pairs. They have ninety seconds to write down as many currencies as they can. Compare answers as a class and check that students know in which country or countries each currency is used.

Read the tip box in the margin. Ask students why these abbreviations are useful. (They are international and save confusion, especially with currencies that have the same name in different countries.) Students match the abbreviations with the currencies and countries.

1	RUR	rouble	Russia
2	USD	dollar	USA
3	THB	baht	Thailand
4	NZD	dollar	New Zealand
5	EUR	Euro	Eurozone countries
6	GBP	pound	the UK
7	MXN	peso	Mexico
8	PLN	zloty	Poland
9	ZAR	rand	South Africa

Exercise 5, page 93

Students often have problems saying and understanding big numbers. Before reading out the numbers from the bill, ask students to practise saying them in pairs. They then listen and repeat after you.

> In UK English, people usually say *two hundred **and** thirty-five* while in US English it is usually *two hundred thirty-five*. In both UK and US English there is no *and* after *thousand*, e.g. *one thousand two hundred*.

Professional practice: Preparing bills

Ask students some comprehension questions about preparing bills so that they read the checklist carefully.

1 *Why should you avoid hidden charges?*
2 *What should always be on display?*
3 *What other things should you include on the bill?*
4 *How should you deal with bill queries?*
5 *Why is it a good idea to check hotel records?*
6 *What should you do if there has been a mistake?*

Exercise 6, page 93

Students do a role-play between a hotel receptionist and a guest who is checking out. The guest queries the bill.

Elicit the start of the conversation and write on the board if necessary:

A: Are you checking out now sir / madam?
B: Yes, that's right. Room …
A: Here's your bill.
B: Just a minute. I think there's been a mistake …

Students practise the dialogue in pairs. Choose volunteers to act out the dialogue in front of the class. Set up a mock reception desk so that the situation is as real as possible. Remember that the receptionists need to be polite and solve the problem so that the guest leaves satisfied.

Students can refer back to the tapescript on page 142 of the students' book if necessary.

Exercise 7, page 94

The vocabulary in this exercise is very specific to the hotel industry and so some words, such as *upsell* and *flat charge* might not be found in a standard dictionary. Students work in pairs and use dictionaries to match the words with the definitions. Students should be encouraged to guess the meaning of any words they cannot find in the dictionary or to ask you for help.

> *Upselling* is an important sales technique in the hospitality industry whereby existing customers are encouraged to upgrade and pay for more profitable facilities and services.

1 b **2** h **3** c **4** f **5** g **6** e **7** d **8** a

Exercise 8, page 94

Tell students that they are going to read a text about upselling at registration. It gives hotels / hotel staff advice on how to upsell and the reasons for doing it. Students should read the questions and predict possible answers in pairs before reading the text. Students then read the text and answer the questions, underlining the relevant information in the text. *Did you predict any answers correctly?*

1 The hotel loses money.
2 If the reservation was made by a travel agent or secretary.
3 Business travellers might need more work space, or guests are sometimes tired after a long journey.
4 Find out whether the guest knows about them. Present upgrades as a unique opportunity. Mention higher rates to show lower rates as good value.
5 Corporate rates.

Language focus: Conditional 1

Before looking at the explanation on page 95, write the three examples given in the language focus on the board. Elicit the structure of each sentence. Elicit when each form is used. Ask students whether there is any difference between the second and third. (No.) Students check their answers with the language focus or refer to the grammar reference on page 130 of the students' book.

Emphasise that the so-called *zero conditional* (*if* + present + present) is used to talk about facts / things that are always true while *conditional 1* (*if* + present + modal verb + infinitive) is used to make predictions / assumptions.

See grammar reference section (students' book pages 130–131).

Exercise 9, page 95

Tell students that they are going to read a webpage about upgrading rooms. Give them true / false questions so that they read through the whole text first to get the general meaning.

1 *There are special discounts for the most expensive rooms.* (F)
2 *Sometimes it is not worth paying extra.* (T)
3 *Often there is a 'flat charge' for upgrading.* (T)

Now read the text again and fill in the gaps. Sometimes more than one answer is possible.

1 is **2** costs **3** pays / will pay **4** is offered **5** has / will have **6** is **7** is always / will always be **8** also benefits / will also benefit

Exercise 10, page 95

In this exercise students practise conditional 1. It creates a chain of predictions based on the information in the text.

- If we upsell at registration, guests will upgrade rooms.
- If guests upgrade rooms, they will be happier.
- If guests are happier, they will re-book.
- If guests re-book, the hotel will make more money.
- If the hotel makes more money, the staff will earn commission.
- If the staff earn commission, they will be happier / work harder, etc.

Extra Activity
1 Continue the chain in exercise 10 in pairs and see what results they give.
2 Start a new chain beginning with: *If hotel staff are polite and efficient, guests will ...*
In pairs, students make a chain of predictions with four more conditional sentences.

Workbook homework: exercises 5 and 6, page 58.

Exercise 11, page 95

Tell students that they are going to role-play a variety of situations. Student A is the receptionist and student B is various guests with different requirements checking in at the hotel. Student B begins each time and tells the receptionist what he / she wants according to the instructions on page 124. The receptionist responds according to the instructions on page 122. Choose volunteers to act out their role-play(s) to the rest of the class. Set up the classroom to resemble a hotel reception desk.

Exercise 12, page 96

Tell students that they are going to hear a receptionist upselling to a guest who is leaving the hotel. Students should read the questions carefully before listening to the CD / cassette and then listen twice before comparing their answers with a partner. Check answers as a class. Ask what they think of the receptionist's manner. *Is he good at upselling? What about the guest: how does she respond?*

1 He asks the guest whether she is planning to return to St Petersburg.
2 An advance booking for June.
3 He makes the festival sound interesting, and emphasises the need to book well in advance.
4 No, the guest will ask her PA to confirm.
5 A mini-suite for an extra $20.
6 He offers to book tickets for the festival.

Extra Activity
To simplify the listening task for less advanced students, give true / false statements.
1 *The guest is plannning to come back on holiday in June.*
2 *The receptionist tells the guest about a festival in July.*
3 *He makes the festival sound interesting and attractive.*
4 *The woman re-books immediately.*
5 *The mini-suite is an extra $20.*
6 *The receptionist also offers to book the woman some tickets for the festival.*

Exercise 13, page 96

Play the CD / cassette again and stop after each phrase so that students have enough time to complete the gaps. Play again without stopping so that they can check their answers.

Students can then practise the dialogues in pairs.

1 I could book it for you **2** So that's **3** departing on **4** For only twenty dollars **5** you'll find it **6** will be happy to **7** Not at all

Exercise 14, page 96

Remind students once again about the importance of politeness when dealing with customers in any situation. When making suggestions it is also important to sound enthusiastic as this will persuade the customer that what you are promoting is worthwhile. This exercise helps with asking questions in an appropriate way. Students listen and repeat after each question, then practise in pairs.

Workbook homework: exercise 8, page 59.

Exercise 15, page 97

Ask students what a *memo* is. Refer them to the memo on page 97 and ask who the memo is for. (All reception desk staff.)

What is the purpose of this memo? (To emphasise to staff how important it is to try and re-book guests before they leave.)

What are staff requested to do with all guests? (To invite guests to book their next reservation at check-out.)

Students read the memo again and complete the gaps using the appropriate form of the verbs in brackets. If necessary, elicit the form of the zero conditional and conditional 1 before completing the gaps. Check answers as a class.

> *memo*: a short official note to another person in the same company or organisation. You can also write a memo to yourself to remind yourself to do something.

1 is **2** will be **3** ask **4** are given **5** invite
6 books / will book

Professional practice: Front-desk staff in sales

Students may be surprised that front-desk staff / receptionists can take responsibility for hotel sales and in some hotels it is considered an extremely important part of their job.

Refer them back to the dialogue in exercise 12: *What did the receptionist try and sell to the guest? How did he do it? What was his manner like?*

Students check the tapescript on page 142 and find appropriate phrases for each point in the professional practice box. They should use these phrases in exercise 16.

Suggested answers
- upsell at check out:
  Do you know there's a festival in June? Guests usually book six months in advance.
- re-book guests at check-out:
  If you like, I could book it for you now. It won't take a minute.
- point out the value of the room rate:
  For only $20 more, I can book you a mini-suite. I'm sure you'll find it more comfortable for meetings.
- offer information about hotel facilities:
  Here's a programme. You can fax me and our concierge will be happy to book them for you.

Exercise 16, page 97

In this exercise, students role-play a situation between a guest checking out and a receptionist re-booking and upselling. Put students into pairs. Give them enough time to read their instructions and to decide what they need to say and what expressions they can use. Student A invents the additional charges and the festivals or events. Remind students to be polite, especially the receptionists.

Workbook homework: exercise 4, page 58 and exercise 7, page 59.

> **Extra Activity**
> Ask students whether they would feel confident about dealing with queries at reception. What would they find difficult about it? *What qualities / skills do you need? What are the most important things to remember when dealing with bill queries and upselling to guests?*

P Photocopiable extra, see page 91

This activity revises functional language and situations that are covered throughout the course.

Divide students into groups of three and give each group a set of situation cards cut up and placed face down. Tell students that each card has a situation on it which corresponds to a context that they have studied during the course. They read the situation and respond to it saying what they would say / do in each situation.

Student A picks up a card and reads the situation to the person on their left (student B). If student B gives an appropriate answer, B keeps the card; if the answer is not appropriate or B does not give any answer, student C has the chance to answer. If C's answer is correct C keeps the card. Now student B picks up a card and repeats the procedure. Continue in this way until all the cards have been used (or set a time limit). The winner is the student who has the most cards at the end.

Winds of change

UNIT OBJECTIVES

Professional practice: giving weather information, giving presentations
Language focus: tense review: past, present and future forms
Vocabulary: weather conditions

Fact File

Dorling Kindersley Eyewitness Travel Guide Mexico
Websites: http://travel.dk.com, www.mexconnect.com

Unit notes

Ask students what they know about Mexico: its landscape, culture, history and tourist attractions. *Would you like to go there on holiday?*

Fact File

Although, geographically, Mexico is part of North rather than Central America, it is generally thought of as a Central American country. Its capital, Mexico City, is one of the most densely populated cities in the world. The numerous monuments around the country, built by ancient civilisations such as the Aztecs and Mayans, are the main tourist attractions, but Mexico also offers opportunities for walking with its great variety of landscape. A different side of tourism is also available for people who just want to lie on a beautiful sandy beach.
Amongst the top sites in Mexico are the Mayan settlement in Palenque, the Pyramids of Teotihuacán and the Yucatán Peninsula.

Exercise 1, page 98

Students discuss the questions in pairs. Before they start, make sure they know the question *What's the weather like?*, and elicit the seasons (*spring, summer, autumn, winter*). Compare answers as a class. Ask them whether they like the weather in their country or if they would prefer to live somewhere with a different climate. *Which is your favourite season? Why?*

Exercise 2, page 98

Look at the information on page 99 before looking at the questions. Ask students whether there is much variety in the climate around Mexico, so that they scan the information during the first reading and just get the gist of the text. Students then look at the information again and answer the questions. *Is there as much variety in the climate and landscape in your country?*

1 Veracruz 2 Chihuahua 3 Acapulco 4 Mérida
5 Acapulco 6 desert

Exercise 3, page 98

Before looking at the symbols in the book, ask students what typical symbols are used in television / newspaper weather forecasts. Students can draw the symbols on the board for classmates to call out in English. Students then match the symbols with the words from the box.

1 heavy rain 2 cloudy / overcast 3 showers 4 sunshine
5 snow 6 strong winds

Exercise 4, page 98

The words in this exercise are different types of weather. Look at the words first before reading the definitions. Students define the words they know in their own words then match the words with their definitions. After checking answers, ask students whether they have experienced all of these weather conditions. *Is anyone scared of thunder, lightning or floods?*

1 b 2 c 3 a 4 f 5 g 6 e 7 d

> The pronunciation of some weather words is quite difficult. Help students with the pronunciation.
> *hurricane* /ˈhʌrɪ̩kən/
> *thunder* /ˈθʌndə/
> *lightning* /ˈlaɪtnɪŋ/
> *flood* /flʌd/
> *frost* /frɒst/
> *shower* /ˈʃaʊə/

Workbook homework: exercises 3 and 4, pages 60–61.

Exercise 5, page 99

In this exercise, students practise asking basic *yes / no* questions. Elicit which questions they can ask each other to help guess the town / region. *Is it in the north / south / east / west? Is it usually rainy / warm /* etc. *there? Does it have a lot of rain?* Give them a limit of ten questions to guess the location. Practise as long as necessary.

Professional practice: Describing the weather

As well as actual weather words like *rainy, sunny,* etc., it is also useful to know certain phrases to describe weather conditions. Read the phrases as a class and check that students understand their meaning. Students write down the phrases in their notes so that they have their own reference when they need it.

Travel guide project

The climate of your country
In groups, students can produce a section for their travel guides similar to *The Climate of Mexico* from the Dorling Kindersley guide. This should be based on a map of the country and describe average temperatures, rainfall and hours of sunshine throughout the year.

Exercise 6, page 99

Tell students that they are going to hear the weather forecast for five different cities in Mexico. Students look at the map, listen and mark the weather with the symbols from exercise 4. If necessary, tell them which towns they have to mark. Students listen twice and then compare answers in pairs. They then describe the weather in each place as if they were the weather forecasters, using *will*. Compare ideas about the best and worst place to be. Answers will vary depending on students' weather preferences.

Mexico City: storms
Chihuahua: overcast but hot
Guadalajara: heavy rain
Acapulco: heavy rain, humid, hot
Mérida: hot, sunny

Suggested answer for best place: Mérida because it is sunny and it is not raining. Worst place: Mexico City because of the heavy storms.

Workbook homework: exercises 1 and 2, pages 60–61.

Exercise 7, page 99

Set this exercise for homework. Students go home and check the weather forecast for their area for the following day from the TV, a newspaper or the internet. Students present their weather forecasts and compare their answers in the next class.

Extra Activity
Either give each student a different area of their country or ask them to choose a country they are interested in. Students go home and find out the forecast for this area / country for the next few days. Students present their weather forecasts to the class as if they were TV weather forecasters on the news. If you have access to a map of the country or a world map, stick it on the board so that students can point to the places as they give their forecasts. If you have time, make some weather symbols on card which they can put on the map.

Exercise 8, page 100

Students look at the pictures and describe them in pairs. *What impression do you get of Mexico from these pictures? Would you like to see these things?*

Read the topics in the box and ask what information they would expect to hear in reference to each topic, e.g. dates when talking about history, nightclubs and shows when talking about entertainment, etc. This will help them when they listen for the first time.

Students listen and match the extracts with the topics. When checking answers, students say what clues helped them to get their answers.

1 landscape **2** history **3** economy

Exercise 9, page 100

Before listening again, students should read the questions carefully. They listen twice before comparing their answers with a partner. Check answers as a class and discuss the information about Mexico. *What do you find interesting?* Ask them to describe the landscape. *Would you like to know more about the Mayan civilisation? What do you think of the tourism industry's plan? Having listened to this information, would you like to go there on holiday?*

If they are interested in Mexico and the Mayan civilisation and want to find out more, refer them to *Dorling Kindersley Eyewitness Travel Guide Mexico* or to www.mexconnect.com.

1 over half of the country
2 tropical, green and fertile with rainforests
3 astronomy
4 before the arrival of the Spanish conquistadors in the sixteenth century
5 over twenty million
6 increase number of hotel rooms by twenty percent, and improve airports, public transport, restaurants and recreational facilities

Language focus: Tense review 1: Present and past forms

Students match the examples with the rules. Check as a class and refer students to the grammar reference on pages 125–127 of the students' book if necessary.

1 a 2 d 3 c 4 b 5 e

Exercise 10, page 101

In this exercise, students learn more interesting facts about Mexico as well as practising the grammar. Before completing the sentences they should decide whether a present or past form is required and then choose the correct form, referring to the language focus box on page 100 of the students' book for help. While checking answers, students comment on any information they find interesting in the sentences.

1 was 2 is celebrated 3 were used 4 have opened
5 are often visited 6 be seen 7 has been

Workbook homework: exercises 5 and 6, pages 62–63.

Language focus: Tense review 2: Future forms

Before looking at the language focus, either elicit the four future forms and their uses or write examples of each form on the board and ask students to discuss in pairs when each tense is used. Check answers with the information in the box.

See grammar reference section (students' book pages 128–129).

Exercise 11, page 101

Tell students that they are going to complete a text about marriage and honeymoons (check the understanding of *honeymoon*). Ask students to look at the picture of the honeymoon couple and to describe it in pairs.

Before reading the text, ask students where people in their country normally go on honeymoon and what activities they usually do. *Where would you like to go when / if you get married?*

Extra Activity

Treat the text as a reading comprehension as well as a grammar exercise. Ask these questions so that they read the whole text:

1 *In what ways are modern honeymoons different from those of the past?* (People now go abroad on honeymoon.)
2 *What do honeymoon packages include?* (The wedding and the honeymoon.)
3 *Which two destinations are popular with honeymooners?* (The Caribbean and Mexico.)
4 *Why do people want to do something different for their honeymoon?* (To do something special / exciting / memorable.)
5 *What do you think about getting married away from home?* (Students give their own answers.)

Students now complete the text with the correct form. Look for clues to help them decide which form is necessary. Sometimes more than one answer is possible.

1 are changing / have changed 2 didn't go 3 has been
4 want 5 go / are going 6 has been 7 started
8 are going to buy / are buying 9 won't change
10 will continue

go abroad: go to another country
trend: fashion
all-inclusive: including everything
spend money on something

Workbook homework: exercise 7, page 63.

Exercise 12, page 102

Look at the types of tourism mentioned in the vocabulary box. Ask students what they understand by these terms. Students look at the pictures of the tourists and match them with the types of tourism. In pairs, students describe the different types of tourism and say what people generally do on these types of trips. *Which type of tourism is most common in your country?*

1 business travel 2 ecotourism 3 mass tourism

Exercise 13, page 102

Tell students that they are going to hear three tourists describing their trips to Mexico. Their experiences are quite different. Students should read the questions carefully before listening. They then listen and complete the answers.

1 third tourist **2** first tourist **3** third tourist **4** first tourist **5** second tourist **6** second tourist

- The first tourist talks about the present and uses present simple.
- The second tourist talks about the past and uses past simple.
- The third tourist talks about the future and uses present simple, past simple, present perfect, present continuous and *going to*.

Extra Activity

To exploit the listening text further, ask more detailed questions about the trips:

1 *How often does the first tourist go to Mexico City?* (About once a month.)
2 *Why does he need a relaxing hotel?* (He travels a lot.)
3 *What does he usually buy?* (Ceramics or rugs.)
4 *Where did the second tourist go two years ago?* (Guatemala and southern Mexico.)
5 *Where are the best ruins?* (In the jungle.)
6 *What was the climate like there?* (Really hot and humid.)
7 *Where does the third tourist usually go?* (Spain or a European city.)
8 *Where are they going on their honeymoon?* (Cancún.)
9 *How long after the wedding are they flying from Madrid?* (Two days.)

Exercise 14, page 102

Students discuss the questions in pairs first. Then each pair joins another pair to make groups of four and share ideas. They do not need to agree with each other; the more ideas they have the better. Alternatively, set the questions for homework beforehand so that they have time to go away and research the information a little. They can check with the tourist office, the town council or the internet and then discuss what information they have found in class with a partner.

Travel guide project

Changes and development in tourism in your country
After students have discussed the questions in pairs, they write an article based on the information they discussed. They add these articles to their projects.

Workbook homework: exercise 8, page 63.

Exercise 15, page 103

Students look at the pictures of the holidays and in pairs describe what is shown. As well as describing the pictures, students should discuss the following: *What kind of tourism is illustrated in each picture? Which places are most / least exploited? How can each place be best developed? Is it possible to develop a place for tourism without destroying it? Should there be stricter laws on how much a natural area can be exploited? Why?*

Ask students how much their country has been developed for tourism over the years. *Have any places been ruined? How? Are there any restrictions on development in any parts of the country? Are there any undeveloped areas that would be good places to develop tourism? Why would they make a good location?*

Tell students that they are going prepare a tourist development project in groups for an undeveloped area of their country. If they have problems choosing a suitable location, help them choose one.

Before they start to plan the projects in groups, they should look at the information on page 103 of the students' book and the checklist of points to include in their proposal.

spending power: the amount of spending money that people have available

When they present their projects they will need to include as much detail as possible. They can invent any information that they do not know. Tell groups that they are free to develop their area in any way they want, as long as the plan is realistic and viable. Give them plenty of time to prepare and revise their proposal.

Once they have their plans ready, refer them to the professional practice box on page 103. Read through the useful tips and give the groups extra time to prepare how they are going to present their projects to the rest of the class. Give them a context for the presentations, e.g. *You are going to present your development plan to the National Tourist Board. They would like to develop two new areas of tourism in the next three years and are looking for prospective development projects. Present your plans to the board.*

While each group gives their presentation, the rest of the class act as the tourist board, asking any questions where appropriate. The board votes for the two most viable projects. Spend time on feedback on the projects. Discuss the viability of each project and the potential success of each one in boosting tourism in the country.

Travel guide project

A tourism development project for …
Students write up the development plans as formal written documents and add them to their projects.

Extra Activity

Ask students to discuss briefly the future of tourism in their country. *Is it likely to increase / decrease in the next ten years? Why? What is the trend in your country: to go abroad or to stay in the country? Why? Is this trend likely to change in the next ten years?*

P. Photocopiable extra, see page 92

The two extra activities in this unit serve as a grammar and vocabulary review of all the units. They are useful and enjoyable activities to do at the end of the course.

Grammar Auction

This game is a whole class activity but students can choose their answers in pairs.

Introduce the idea of an auction. Ask students what it is and what happens there. *Has anyone been to one or seen one on TV?* Introduce useful auction expressions like *auctioneer, make a bid* and *Going to the man / lady at the front. Going, going, gone.* (This is what the auctioneer says when the last person has made their bid to make it clear who has 'won' the item on sale – in this case, a sentence!)

Tell them that instead of money, each pair has air miles to spend. Tell students about Air Miles: in the UK some companies and services are affiliated with Air Miles. As a result, customers can earn air miles when they shop in a particular supermarket, stay in a hotel, use a credit card, etc. The air miles are 'saved' in an account and can later be used to pay for flights. Ask students whether there is anything similar in their country. (See www.airmiles.co.uk for more information.)

Give a copy of the sentences to each pair and tell them that some of the sentences are grammatically correct but others are not. The aim of the game is to identify whether or not each sentence is correct and to bet with air miles on the ones they think are correct. The winners are the group with the most air miles at the end. They will then be able to choose a destination anywhere in the world within the range of their air miles.

Each pair has a maximum of 500 air miles to spend. They can bet with a minimum of 50 air miles on each sentence. The bets should be multiples of ten. The maximum bet at any time is 100 air miles. If they guess correctly they double their stake. If they guess incorrectly they lose their stake. If they can correct an incorrect sentence, they get a bonus 50 air miles.

Students decide in pairs which ones are correct and how many air miles they want to bet on these sentences. Tell them not to bet anything on a sentence they know is incorrect! They write down the number of air miles next to the sentences. They cannot change this figure once the bid for that sentence has started. When they are ready, the auction can begin.

The auction procedure: as in a real auction, the auctioneer (the teacher) reads out the first item and begins with 50 air miles. Read out each sentence as if it is correct and ask whether anyone wants to bid. If so, they put up their hands or make a gesture to show that they are interested and say how much they bid. They can start lower than the number of air miles they have put on their sentence sheet and work up to their final figure. When the final bid has been made, raise your hand and say 'Going to the man / lady with … Going, going, gone.' This adds an authentic touch to the game. Make a note of the pair who has won each sentence and how many air miles they paid for it to check at the end of the game.

It is a good idea for the auctioneer to read out the first few sentences in order and then choose them at random so that the students are kept on their toes. If possible keep up a good pace to make the game more exciting and motivating.

At the end of the game, each pair adds up the number of air miles they have won to see who are the winners. They choose their destination. The runners up can also choose a destination within their total air mile range. If you want to include everyone in a trip somewhere, let each pair choose a destination, even if it is a nearby town!

The correct sentences are 1, 4, 5, 6, 9, 11, 14, 15, 19 and 20.

The incorrect sentences should be:
2 The atmosphere is as friendly as before.
3 Jane knows a good travel agent.
7 If we upsell at registration, guests will be very happy.
8 Picasso's family moved to Barcelona in 1895.
10 You mustn't stand up at take-off.
12 You shouldn't take large amounts of money. (no *to* after *should*)
13 I look forward to hearing from you.
16 The metro system in Istanbul is going to be extended.
17 What are you doing this summer?
18 Avoid wearing expensive jewellery on the street.

P. Photocopiable extra, see page 93–94

Snakes and Ladders

Divide the class into groups of four (two pairs) and give each group a copy of the Snakes and Ladders board, a set of vocabulary cards (cut up, faced down in a pile), a die and a counter for each pair.

Each pair in the group take it in turns to throw the die. If pair A lands on a grey square, pair B takes a vocabulary card and reads out a definition of the word on the card. If pair A gives the correct word they stay on the square, if not they go back to the square they came from. And so on.

If a pair lands at the bottom of a ladder, they must get the correct answer before they can go up it. If they land at the mouth of a snake, they must go all the way down it.

The winners are the first pair to get to the last square (FINISH). They must throw the exact number to reach the last square and they must answer a final question.

When the game is over, either play again to finish off the vocabulary cards or students go through the remaining cards and check the vocabulary.

Consolidation 3

Unit notes

The first page (exercises 1–5) revises and checks the main grammar and vocabulary from units 11–15 and provides further translation practice. These can be set for homework, used as a test in class or done in pairs in class.

The second spread of the consolidation is a review board game which revises all the situations, much of the language and many of the expressions that have been studied during the course. It provides students with a lot of speaking practice and is an enjoyable way to finish the course. Make sure you leave time at the end of the course to use it.

Exercise 1, page 104

Briefly elicit the different uses of the present simple and present continuous before students do the exercise. To make sure that they read the whole text before they start filling in the gaps, ask *Is the writer on holiday or on business?* (business); *How long does he / she want to stay at the hotel?* (definitely three nights; possibly more).

Refer students to the language focus on pages 100 and 101, and to the grammar reference (students' book page 125).

> 1 arrives 2 do not check in 3 does it finish
> 4 am meeting 5 taking 6 plan / am planning
> 7 do not tell 8 am staying

Exercise 2, page 104

Elicit the structure of the present and past simple passive before students do the exercise. Ask students the following questions so that they read the content of the text before they do the exercise itself:

What do hotels want to save? (water and energy)

Give three examples of changes that hotels have made. (plants in public areas, recycled stationery, linen not changed every day, new design in restaurant / bar areas)

In which two ways can hotels benefit from these changes? (save money, good for public relations).

Refer students to the language focus on page 83 and to the grammar reference (students' book page 130).

> 1 are promoted 2 were reduced 3 were put 4 were installed 5 are left 6 is put 7 is not changed 8 are asked 9 are invited 10 were redesigned

Exercise 3, page 105

This exercise revises conditional 1. Ask students what a *superstition* is. *Are you superstitious?* Students give examples of how they are superstitious. Elicit the structure of conditional 1 before students complete the exercise.

Refer students to the language focus on page 95 and to the grammar reference (students' book pages 130–131).

> 1 leave, will come 2 whistle, will lose 3 light, will bring 4 spill, will have, throw

---

Extra Activity

If students are interested in superstitions, they can write examples of superstitions in their own country using the same structure as in the exercise.

Exercise 4, page 105

This exercise revises vocabulary related to tourism and relative clauses. Elicit relative pronouns by asking students to complete the following:

A bill is a thing / something …
A waiter is a person / someone …

Students work in pairs and turn to the relevant pages. They either write definitions before defining the words to their partner or define the words directly without writing them first.

Exercise 5, page 105

In this exercise, students translate a webpage. Before starting the translation, make sure students read the whole text and the tips in the professional practice box. Ask the following general questions before starting:

What is the purpose of the text? (to promote the Buttercup Inn)
What kind of language is used? (descriptive)
What information is given? (list of facilities)
Are any adjectives repeated? (no, so they should use a variety too)

Students write their translations in pairs and then compare with other pairs to see which translation is most suitable.

Professional practice: Translation

Encourage students to follow the tips as they write their translations. It would be useful to find a similar text in their language from a brochure or the internet.

The holiday rep game, pages 106–107

Before setting up the game, give students time to look at the pictures and to describe the situations that they represent. Ask them to discuss which situations they would find most difficult if they were tour operator representatives and what they would do in those situations. *What do the pictures tell us about the job of a rep?* (that they have to deal with a lot of different situations, many of which are problematic)

Setting up the game:

The game is best played in pairs or groups of three so that each student has the opportunity to speak a lot and no one has to wait too long for their next turn. To make the most of the game, use a coin instead of a die. If students throw heads, they move one space; if they throw tails they move two.

Tell students that when they land on a square, they should read the situation carefully and follow the instructions. If they land on a square which requires them to describe, sell, complain, etc., they should decide what is the most appropriate thing to say and the most appropriate way to say it. Remind them that they must be polite and enthusiastic. If necessary they can help each other. Give them a minute or two to read quickly through the information on the squares and to ask any questions if they do not understand something. Now they are ready to start!

Depending on how long they take to complete the game and how much they enjoy it, change pairs / groups and repeat. If they land on some of the same squares, they should try to use a different way to answer.

After playing the game, would you like to be a rep?

Useful language for playing games:
* *Whose turn is it?*
* *It's my / your turn.*
* *What do I / you have to do?*
* *Go back … / Move forward … space.*
* *Don't cheat!*

Unit 1: Hotel jobs and duties

housekeeper	I greet guests at the door. I sometimes collect guests and luggage from the airport.
hotel manager	I serve food and drinks to guests and train new staff.
bartender	I do all the hotel's finances.
accountant	I clean the guestrooms. I make the beds and change the sheets.
concierge	I serve guests at the bar.
porter	I don't work at the hotel. I'm on holiday.
waiter	I carry guests' bags to their rooms.
marketing manager	I manage all the hotel staff.
receptionist	I serve guests in the restaurant.
head waiter	I find business for the hotel. I organise advertising the hotel.
guest	I work behind the front desk. I welcome guests when they arrive and give them their keys.

Unit 3: Food and restaurant word puzzles

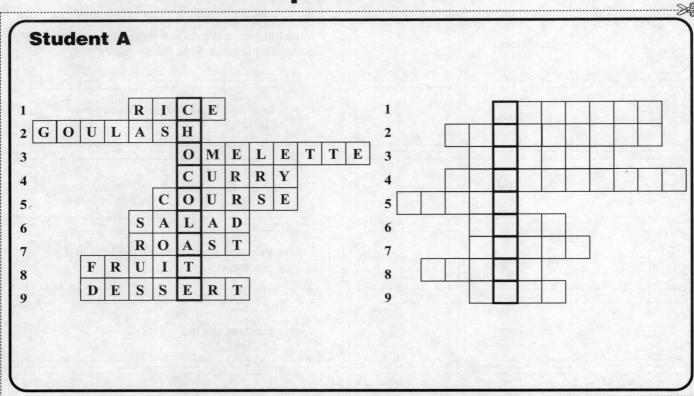

Student A

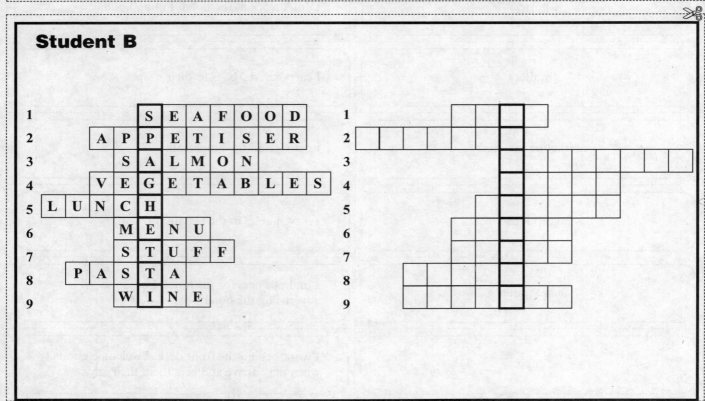

Student B

Unit 4: Giving directions

Student A Barcelona Old Town

Ask your partner politely where the following places are and complete the key below:

Museums and Galleries
- **2** The Picasso Museum (Museu Picasso)
- **4** The Museum of Contemporary Art
- ● Museu Marítim
- ● Museu d'Art Modern

Streets and Districts
- **1** La Rambla
- **5** The Old Port (Port Vell)
- ● Monument a Colom
- ● Plaça Reial

Churches
- **6** Barcelona Cathedral
- ● Basílica de Santa Maria del Mar

Historic Buildings
- **7** Palau de la Música Catalana
- ● Casa de la Ciuitat

Parks and Gardens
- **3** Parc de la Ciutadella
- ● Parc Zoològic

Student B Barcelona Old Town

Start here

Key:
- Ⓜ Metro Station
- 🚉 Train Station
- 🚌 Main Bus Stop
- ℹ Tourist Information
- Ⓟ Parking

Universitat

Catalunya

Urquinaona

Arc de Triomf

PLAÇA DE VICENS MARTORELL

PLAÇA DE LA VILA DE MADRID

PLAÇA DE SANT PERE

BUENAVENTURA MUÑOZ

CARRER DE JOAQUIN COSTA

CARRER DELS TALLERS

CARRER DE PELAI

CARRER DEL CARME

CARRER DE L'HOSPITAL

LA RAMBLA

Liceu

PLAÇA D'ANTONI MAURA

VIA LAIETANA

SANT PERE MES BAIX

PLAÇA DE SANT AGUSTI VELL

CARRER DEL COMERÇ

PASSEIG DE PICASSO

PASSEIG DELS TIL·LERS

PARC DE LA CIUTADELLA

PASSEIG DE PU

CARRER DE WELLINGTON

CARRER DE FERRAN

AVINYO

CARRER DE LA PRINCESA

Jaume I

CARRER

PARC ZOOLOGIC

Drassanes

LA RAMBLA

PLAÇA DEL DUC DE MEDINACELI

PASSEIG DE COLOM

PLAÇA D'ANTONI LOPEZ

Estació de França

Barceloneta

PASSEIG DE CIRCUMVAL·LACIO

PLAÇA DE PAU VILA

RONDA DEL LITORAL

DK

Ask your partner politely where the following places are and complete the key below:

Museums and Galleries
- ⬤ The Picasso Museum (Museu Picasso)
- ⬤ The Museum of Contemporary Art
- ⑩ Museu Marítim
- ⑬ Museu d'Art Modern

Streets and Districts
- ⬤ La Rambla
- ⬤ The Old Port (Port Vell)
- ⑫ Monument a Colom
- ⑭ Plaça Reial

Churches
- ⬤ Barcelona Cathedral
- ⑪ Basílica de Santa Maria del Mar

Historic Buildings
- ⬤ Palau de la Música Catalana
- ⑧ Casa de la Ciuitat

Parks and Gardens
- ⬤ Parc de la Ciutadella
- ⑨ Parc Zoològic

Unit 5: Choosing a hotel

Hotels

A: Hotel Amsterdam

Rooms: 80. 🛏 1 🏨 TV 🍸 📋 🛎 ♿ 🔄 🐕 🍸 🍴 💳 *AE, DC, MC, V, JCB.*

Price range: €€€

Facilities: restaurant and bar, wheelchair access, lift, pets allowed, but not children

This charming hotel is at street level, where you can sit all day on the terrace, watching the world go by. The hotel restaurant serves a good buffet breakfast and specialises in Dutch cuisine. All rooms are well equipped but the front rooms are noisy so ask for a room at the back where you will not be disturbed.

B: Grand Sofitel Demeure

Rooms: 182. 🛏 1 🏨 24 TV 🍸 ⚡ 📋 🏊 🛎 🏃 🔄 P 🍸 🍽 🍴 💳 *AE, DC, MC, V, JCB.*

Price range: €€€€€

Facilities: 24 hour room service, restaurant and bar, conference rooms, car park, lift, swimming pool, sauna and gym.

Amsterdam's newest luxury hotel, it occupies one of the most historic locations in the city. The luxurious bedrooms are all beautifully decorated. The restaurant is well-known for its high-quality food.

C: Hotel Avenue

Rooms: 80. 🛏 1 🏨 TV 🏃 ♿ 🔄 🐕 🍸 💳 *AE, DC, MC, V, JCB.*

Price range: €€€

Facilities: breakfast room, bar, wheelchair access, lift, pets allowed.

This six-storey hotel is located in the centre of town. Although traffic disturbs the front rooms, rooms at the back are quiet and those on the upper floors at the back have interesting roof-top views. The small breakfast room and bar downstairs are functional.

D: Amstel Botel

Rooms: 176. 🛏 1 🏨 TV 🔄 🍸 💳 *AE, DC, MC, V, JCB.*

Price range: €€

Facilities: bar, lift.

This big modern boat-hotel located on the River Amstel is the only floating hotel in the city. Although the accommodation is not spacious, it is clean and tidy. Being on the river, the views from the rooms are wonderful.

Price categories for a standard double room per night, including breakfast, tax and service:

€ under €100

€€ €100–€150

€€€ €150–€200

€€€€ €200–€250

€€€€€ more than €250

Guests

A: The Jones family: they are a family of four with two young children. They do not wish to spend too much money on accommodation and would prefer to be in one room.

B: Mr and Mrs Adams: they are an elderly couple with a dog. They want a quiet hotel, which does not allow children to stay. The wife is in a wheelchair.

C: A group of friends who do not want to spend a lot of money. They do not mind sharing one room and would like to be near the water.

D: Mr Smithers: he is a businessman who is in Amsterdam for some meetings. He likes to continue with his exercise routine while he is away on business as it relieves stress. His company are paying for his accommodation.

Follow-up: when you have chosen a hotel for each group of guests, tell your partner(s) which hotel you would prefer to stay at and explain why.

Unit 6: Have you been to the casino yet?

A: You don't like sport and you want a lazy holiday.

Cinema (go) *the last three nights*
Library (go) *yesterday morning to read the newspaper*
Riviera Pool (swim) *no*
Jacuzzi (have) *no*
Tennis (play) *no*
The Captain (speak) *on the first day*
Al Fresco Pizzeria (eat) *on the first night*
Disco (dance) *last night and the night before*
The ship (get off) *no*
Sick (be) *last night after dinner*

B: You are very healthy. You like sport and want an active holiday.

Cinema (go) *once*
Library (go) *no*
Riviera Pool (swim) *twice a day*
Jacuzzi (have) *yesterday*
Tennis (play) *every morning*
The Captain (speak) *this morning*
Al Fresco Pizzeria (eat) *on the first night*
Disco (dance) *no*
The ship (get off) *in Luxor and Karnak*
Sick (be) *of course not*

C: You have felt ill since you arrived on the cruise and don't like being on the ship.

Cinema (go) *no*
Library (go) *yesterday morning*
Riviera Pool (swim) *no*
Jacuzzi (have) *yesterday morning*
Tennis (play) *no*
The Captain (speak) *every day to complain*
Al Fresco Pizzeria (eat) *no*
Disco (dance) *no*
The ship (get off) *at every stop*
Sick (be) *every day*

D: You paid a lot of money for this cruise so you want to do as much as possible.

Cinema (go) *last night and the night before*
Library (go) *yesterday after breakfast*
Riviera Pool (swim) *yesterday and the two previous days*
Jacuzzi (have) *this morning and yesterday morning*
Tennis (play) *this afternoon and yesterday afternoon*
The Captain (speak) *every day*
Al Fresco Pizzeria (eat) *every lunchtime*
Disco (dance) *every night*
The ship (get off) *this morning at Luxor and two days ago at Karnak*
Sick (be) *no*

E: You like meeting new people and playing sport.

Cinema (go) *no*
Library (go) *two days ago*
Riviera Pool (swim) *this morning and yesterday morning and evening*
Jacuzzi (have) *after swimming*
Tennis (play) *before swimming*
The Captain (speak) *on the first day and yesterday*
Al Fresco Pizzeria (eat) *no*
Disco (dance) *last night and the night before*
The ship (get off) *no*
Sick (be) *no*

F: You want to have a relaxing holiday and not to do too much.

Cinema (go) *no*
Library (go) *yesterday morning to read a magazine*
Riviera Pool (swim) *this morning*
Jacuzzi (have) *every day*
Tennis (play) *no*
The Captain (speak) *on the first evening*
Al Fresco Pizzeria (eat) *on the first night*
Disco (dance) *no*
The ship (get off) *no*
Sick (be) *no*

Unit 8: Let's talk about the future

START	Hotels will become more and more luxurious. 11	With the world's climate getting hotter, people will prefer cooler holiday destinations. 12	**GO FORWARD THREE SPACES** 23	In the future people are going to spend less money on travel and more on material goods. 24
Air travel will get cheaper. 1	**HAVE ANOTHER GO** 10	I'm going to work in some area of tourism this summer. 13	Business people are going to travel less and do more virtual business conferencing. 22	**FREE QUESTION** 25
Tourism in my country will increase a lot in the next five years. 2	The weather here is going to be good tomorrow. 9	It will become less dangerous for women to travel alone. 14	Adventure sports holidays will become one of the most popular types of holiday. 21	I'm going to work in the tourism industry when I finish my studies. 26
Man will slowly destroy all the best nature spots in the world. 3	More and more people are going to travel to space. 8	**MISS A TURN** 15	One day I will travel around the world. 20	**GO BACK THREE SPACES** 27
I'm going to pass my final tourism exams. 4	**FREE QUESTION** 7	Eco-friendly holidays will become very popular. 16	In the future people are going to … ? 19	Employees in the tourism industry will always have work. 28
THROW AGAIN 5	People are going to choose more unusual holidays. 6	I'm going to work in a hotel one day. 17	The Caribbean will always be a popular destination. 18	**FINISH**

Unit 9: What would you say?

Someone comes up to you at check-in and asks you if you will take a small package for her grandson who has already gone through to the departure lounge.

You are a security official at the airport. On the camera screen you see that someone has a small knife in their hand luggage.

You are sitting next to someone on the plane who takes out a cigarette and a lighter.

Someone in your family has packed their suitcases but hasn't put any name and address labels on them.

You are a flight attendant. The plane is preparing for take-off and you see a passenger talking on his mobile phone.

At check-in you see that the person you are travelling with still has the destination labels from their previous trip on their luggage.

A friend of yours is going to fly for the first time. Give them some advice.

Your young son wants to take his toy gun on the plane with him.

You are a travel agent. A customer wants to know when to arrive at the airport for an international flight.

You are on a long distance flight. Your travel companion wants to drink as much of the free drink as possible. You do not think it is a good idea.

You are a travel agent. A customer tells you that she is vegetarian and asks about food on the flight.

A colleague of yours at work is taking his lap-top computer with him on a flight. Advise him to back up his software.

The person sitting next to you on the plane is asleep when the plane descends for landing. He is not wearing his seatbelt.

You are a flight attendant in an emergency. One of the passengers is wearing high-heeled shoes.

You are a flight attendant. A passenger sitting next to an emergency exit has a bag next to the exit.

You are a cabin crew member. A friend of yours is going to do the training course to become one too. Tell them what you have to do on the course.

You are a check-in attendant. You notice that the person you are checking in does not have a valid passport.

You are a travel agent. A customer wants to know when to arrive at the airport for a domestic flight.

You are a check-in attendant. Someone has a very heavy bag which they want to take as hand luggage.

You are a flight attendant. A very difficult passenger refuses to fasten his seatbelt during take-off.

Unit 10: Choosing a conference venue

You work for a large multi-national company. You are looking for a weekend conference venue for 500 delegates from around the world, some of whom have a low level of English. You want a comfortable venue that is easily accessible and provides a range of equipment and facilities. This is an important business conference which also requires an element of entertainment and relaxation outside the conference time.

You are not interested in how much it will cost at this stage. You just want to know what facilities are on offer.

You work for a large multi-national company. You are looking for a weekend conference venue for 500 delegates from around the world, some of whom have a low level of English. You want a comfortable venue which will offer suitable conditions for a successful and stress-free conference. As well as the conference facilities themselves, you are also interested in providing the delegates with the chance to relax and socialise in the evenings.

You are not interested in how much it will cost at this stage. You just want to know what facilities are on offer.

Central Hotel

Business and Conference Centre
Cardiff
Located in the centre of the city, the hotel is easily accessible. We have a large, well-lit and airy conference room, with top-of-the-range equipment facilities to cater for all your needs.

The Conference Suite
This is the largest suite at the hotel which can cater for up to 500 delegates. It is located on the ground floor and can be divided into two separate rooms if necessary. There is also a private terrace for buffet lunches and break periods.

Other features include air conditioning, bar with lounge area and large dance floor, parking facilities. Swimming pool.

Conferencing equipment
Audiovisual equipment, video-conferencing equipment, overhead projector, slide projector, microphones, flip charts, satellite link, internet access and computer rental.

Support services at your disposal
Secretarial services, printing service, interpreters, photographers, florist and catering services.

Park Hotel

Conference and Leisure Centre
Cardiff
We offer unique, dramatic and tranquil surroundings for conferences, corporate entertainment, team building and training.

We have roomy conference facilities with top-of-the-range equipment.

The Tower Suite
This suite is a large conference and banqueting space which can cater for up to 500 delegates. It overlooks beautiful gardens and a river, offering privacy and tranquillity for your conferences and meetings.

Other features include air-conditioning, private rooms, bar with lounge area and large dance floor. Gym and sauna.

Conferencing equipment
Audiovisual equipment, video-conferencing equipment, overhead projector, slide projector, microphones, flip charts, internet access, direct telephones in conference room.

Support services at your disposal
Secretarial services, conference coordinator, printing service, photographers and catering services.

Unit 12: Selling ski extras

A: You represent Sunshine Tours

1 Sunset descent: descend the slopes with the setting sun. A warm drink will be ready for you when you arrive. $25
2 Snowboarding: includes snowboard hire and two lessons. $45
3 Cross-country skiing: half a day. Includes ski hire and picnic lunch. $35
4 Skiing lessons every morning. $20 per lesson
5 Karaoke night: competition and prizes. $12
6 Dinner and entertainment: live entertainment with comedians and dancers while you dine. Includes three-course meal and entertainment. $60
7 Farewell party: dance the night away to 60s and 70s disco music. Includes buffet and drink. $40

C: You represent Thornhill Holidays

1 Skiing lessons every afternoon. $20 per lesson.
2 Sunset descent: descend the slopes as the sun sets. Fantastic views. Includes a warm drink and a souvenir photo. $30
3 Snowmobile tour: half-day tour through the forest. Includes hire of snowmobile for two people and picnic lunch. $50
4 Snowshoeing: three-hour walk to impressive views. Includes hire of shoes and drink and snack half way. $30
5 Quiz night: participate in a general knowledge quiz and win fantastic prizes. Includes entry, prizes for everyone and one drink. $15
6 Live entertainment: comedians and magicians. $20
7 Farewell dinner and dance: three-course meal followed by dancing to live jazz-swing band. $60

B: You represent Ski with Fun Tours

1 Torchlight procession: ski down the slopes at night with the light of the moon and your torches. Includes a drink and a snack at the end. $30
2 Skiing lessons every morning. $22 per lesson.
3 Cross-country tour: whole day. Includes ski hire and picnic lunch and tea. There will be warm drinks! $45
4 Sledging: hire a sledge and have fun with your friends. $12 for sledge hire per hour.
5 Trivial pursuit quiz night: includes entry, prizes and your first drink. $15
6 Live music night: dance to three local bands. Happy hour from 8–9pm. $18
7 Farewell party: buffet dinner and disco. $40

D: You represent Snow Holiday Tours

1 Skiing lessons every afternoon. $22 per lesson.
2 Torchlight procession: ski down the slopes at midnight. Includes a light meal before descending. $25
3 Snowboarding: includes snowboard hire and one lesson. $35
4 Snowmobile tour: three-hour tour of the slopes. Includes snowmobile hire and light snack.$50
5 Fancy-dress competition: dress up in a costume of your choice. Fantastic prizes for all participants. Includes entry to competition, prizes and surprises. $20
6 Dinner and live music: listen to a local orchestra as you have your dinner. Includes three-course dinner and music. $50
7 Farewell party: buffet supper with live band to follow. Includes food, drink and a small souvenir to take home with you. $35

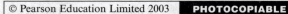

Unit 13: What's the matter with you?

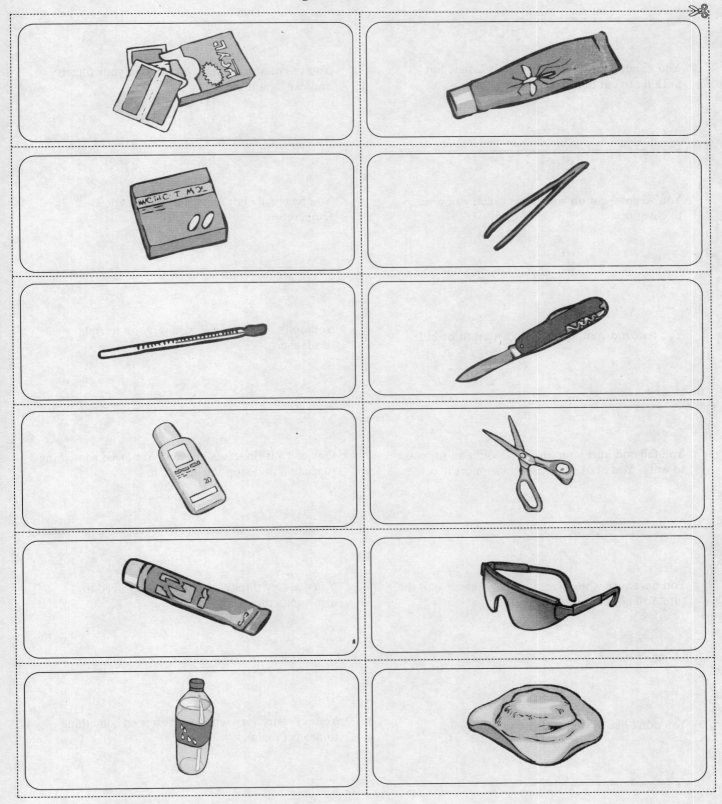

Unit 13: What do you need?

You've cut your finger. You have plasters but nothing to cut them with.

You've got a small piece of wood in your finger and can't get it out.

You've got a cut on your knee which you want to cover up.

You feel really hot and think you've got a temperature.

You hate mosquitoes and don't want to be bitten.

You don't feel very well; you've got a terrible headache.

You fell and hurt your ankle. It's difficult for you to walk. You need something to support it.

One of your fingers is infected. You need something to clean it and stop the infection.

You have very white skin; it's really sensitive to the sun. You need strong protection.

You are very thirsty. You desperately need to drink something.

You don't like having the sun on your head.

Your eyes are very sensitive. You need something to protect them.

Unit 14: What do you do / say?

You are a waiter. A customer complains that their food is cold. What do you say?
Suggested answer: I'll ask the chef to heat it up.

You work for a travel agency. A customer has written to you to complain about their safari holiday. You write a letter of apology. What do you say to show your sympathy? *Suggested answer: I am very sorry that you were unhappy with your holiday.*

You are a waiter. Some customers tell you that there's an extra bottle of wine on the bill. Apologise and explain that there's been a mistake.
Suggested answer: I'm sorry. I'm afraid there's been a mistake.

You are a flight attendant. Tell passengers not to block the emergency exits.
Suggested answer: You mustn't block the emergency exits.

You work at a travel agent's. The phone rings. Pick it up. Introduce yourself and offer to be of assistance.
Suggested answer: (Your name) speaking. How can I help you?

You work as a ski instructor. Give two instructions to skiers.
Suggested answer: use the imperative, e.g. Be careful not to drop your poles, don't bring wet skis into the hotel, etc.

You are making a phone call to a travel agent's. You want to speak to Gabriella. She is on a different line; ask to speak to her.
Suggested answer: Could you put me through to Gabriella, please?

You work at hotel reception. A guest is checking out. He doesn't agree with the bill. What do you do?
Suggested answer: I'll just check that for you. Oh yes, I do apologise, we have made a mistake..

You have seen an advertisement for a job in the *Times*. What do you say at the beginning of a letter saying where you saw the advertisement?
Suggested answer: I am writing in reply / response to your advertisement in the Times.

What are hotel receptionists supposed to do when guests check out?
Suggested answer: Invite them to book their next reservation / re-book.

You are writing a letter of application for a job. Say that they can interview you any morning.
Suggested answer: I am available for interview every morning.

You are writing a reply to a letter of complaint. What should you include in the letter? Give three examples.
Suggested answer: show sympathy, apologise, give an explanation, promise action, offer compensation.

You work at hotel reception. A couple check in. Offer to have the porter carry their luggage.
Suggested answer: Would you like the porter to help you with your luggage?

When giving a guided tour, the guide should follow some tips. What do the letters PIE represent?
Suggested answer: Be polite, give clear information, sound enthusiastic.

Give advice to some tourists. Tell them not to walk around the city late at night.
Suggested answer: It's best not to walk around the city late at night.

Give three pieces of health advice to someone going to a tropical country. *Suggested answer: Make sure you drink lots of fluids, I recommend you use insect repellent, it's essential to take malaria pills, etc.*

Unit 15: Grammar auction

	Your bid in air miles	Buyer / air miles
1 Darina hardly ever finishes early on Mondays.		
2 The atmosphere is as friendlier as before.		
3 Jane is knowing a good travel agent.		
4 Could I have some juice, please?		
5 Have you ever been to the moon?		
6 Would you mind showing me your passports, please?		
7 If we will upsell at reception, guests are very happy.		
8 Picasso's family have moved to Barcelona in 1895.		
9 Would you like me to call the porter?		
10 You don't have to stand up at take-off.		
11 Walking is the best way to see Amsterdam.		
12 You shouldn't to take large amounts of cash.		
13 I look forward to hear from you.		
14 The Thais, who are Buddhists, have many festivals.		
15 Have you taken your sea-sickness pills yet?		
16 The metro system in Istanbul going to be extended.		
17 What do you do this summer?		
18 Avoid to wear expensive jewellery in the street.		
19 The next train arrives at six-thirty.		
20 Some rooms are reserved for guests who are buying Olympic packages.		

Unit 15: Snakes and ladders

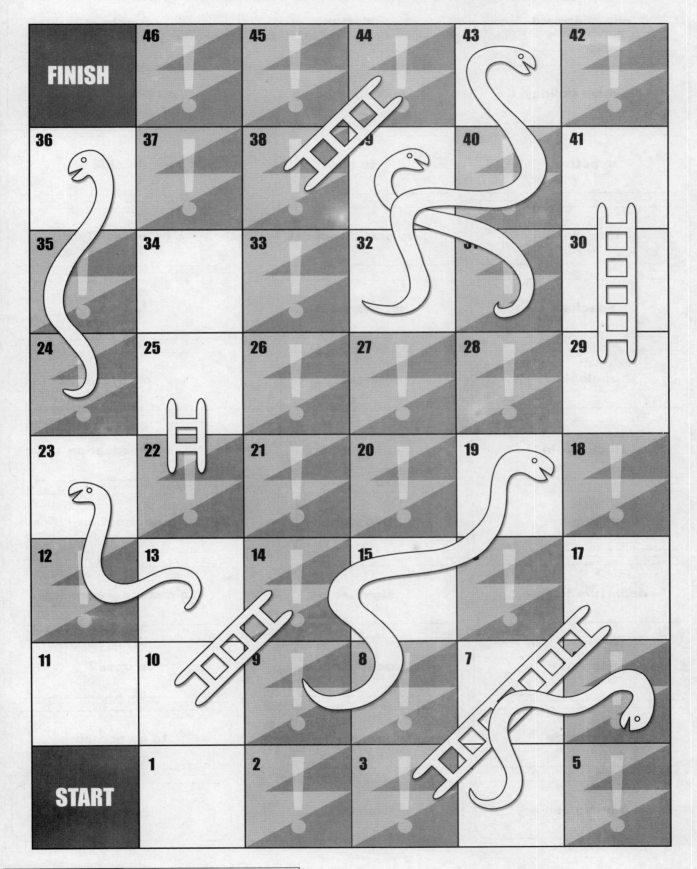

chambermaid	porter	brochure
fly-drive holiday	air conditioning	pick-up location
appetiser	to stuff	the bill
tour guide	to give directions	hotel facilities
spacious	accommodation	luggage
apologise	entertainment	on board
to check in	safety advice	compensation
souvenirs	holidaymaker	destination
departure lounge	sightseeing	to change a booking
insurance	room service	to upsell
to upgrade	landscape	to go abroad
honeymoon	availability	

PHOTOCOPIABLE

天津市版权局著作权合同登记号:图字 02-2007-32。

图书在版编目(CIP)数据

朗文旅游英语初级教师用书 /(英)瑞德(Ridler,E.)
著. —天津:南开大学出版社,2007.6
ISBN 978-7-310-02691-3

Ⅰ.朗… Ⅱ.瑞… Ⅲ.旅游-英语-高等学校-
教学参考资料 Ⅳ.H31

中国版本图书馆 CIP 数据核字(2007)第 044935 号

南开大学出版社出版发行
出版人:肖占鹏
地址:天津市南开区卫津路 94 号　邮政编码:300071
营销部电话:(022)23508339　23500755
营销部传真:(022)23508542　邮购部电话:(022)23502200
*
河北昌黎太阳红彩色印刷有限责任公司印刷
全国各地新华书店经销
*
2007 年 6 月第 1 版　2007 年 6 月第 1 次印刷
889×1194 毫米　16 开本　6 印张　232 千字
定价:18.00 元

如遇图书印装质量问题,请与本社营销部联系调换,电话:(022)23507125